MONSON
Free Library and Reading Room
ASSOCIATION

NO.   63711

RULES AND REGULATIONS

Assessed fines shall be paid by every person keeping Library materials beyond the specified time.

Every person who borrows Library materials shall be responsible for all loss or damage to same while they are out in his name.

All library materials shall be returned to the Library on the call of the Librarian or Directors.

General Laws of Mass., Chap. 266, Sec. 99

Whoever willfully and maliciously or wantonly and without cause writes upon, injures, defaces, tears or destroys a book, plate, picture, engraving or statute belonging to a law, town, city or other public library shall be punished by a fine of not less than five nor more than fifty dollars, or by imprisonment in the jail not exceeding six months.

Dining in America

1850–1900

Dining in America

1850–1900

EDITED BY KATHRYN GROVER

The University of Massachusetts Press

Amherst

and

The Margaret Woodbury Strong Museum

Rochester, New York

1 9 8 7

Copyright © 1987 by The Margaret Woodbury Strong Museum
All rights reserved
Printed in the United States of America
Designed by Barbara Werden
Set in Linoterm Sabon

Library of Congress Cataloging-in-Publication Data

Dining in America, 1850–1900.

Includes index.

1. Dinners and dining—United States—History—19th
century. 2. United States—Social life and customs—
19th century. 3. Cookery, American—History—19th
century. I. Grover, Kathryn, 1953–
GT2853.U5D56   1987   394.1'2'0973   87–5025
ISBN 0–87023–573–7 (alk. paper)
ISBN 0–87023–574–5 (pbk. : alk. paper)

British Library Cataloguing in Publication Data are available.

Contents

Acknowledgments

Collaboration is at the heart of a museum's enterprise, and there is no better testament to that fact than this volume of essays on late nineteenth-century dining. These essays began as papers presented at a Strong Museum symposium on April 26 and 27, 1985, but the symposium itself was preceded by, and born to amplify, an exhibition on American dining conceived in 1983 by Susan R. Williams, curator of household accessories and tablewares. This exhibition, known as *Savory Suppers and Fashionable Feasts,* was the first in the museum's history to be planned and implemented by a team of staff representing the divisions of history, exhibitions, education, and collections. That exhibit team—Mary Lynn Stevens Heininger, Pamela Myers, Florence Smith, and Susan Williams—figured intimately in the success of every part of the project thereafter. *Savory Suppers* is also the first Strong Museum exhibition to travel: the Smithsonian Institution Traveling Exhibition Service (SITES) has taken it on a two-year tour of museums in Albany, New York; Easton, Maryland; Little Rock, Arkansas; Monroe, Louisiana; Yonkers, New York; Norwalk, Connecticut; Ames, Iowa; and San Diego, California.

Education Division Director Marie Hewett helped plan the symposium and organized a group of community representatives—Vivienne Tellier, Jan Hickman, Betty Carlson, Bea

Slizewski, Dorothea Hunter, and Eleanora Church—who also helped in planning the symposium. Florence Smith engineered the entire event with the sincerity, industry, grace, and good cheer we on the Strong Museum staff have come to associate with her. When the papers came to us as manuscripts after the symposium, the hard work on this volume began. Historians Harvey Green, Heininger, and Kasey Grier all acted as in-house readers of the six papers; Strong Museum H. J. Swinney Intern Aleta Zak began and completed much of the involved process of illustration research and requests for permissions before being called away to full-time work in the publications division of the Chicago Historical Society. Melissa Morgan Radtke was, as usual, critical to the smooth execution of photography for the book, and the care with which photographers Michael Radtke and David Cook handled the large number of images necessary to illustrate this book fully is evident in the pages that follow.

Several individuals have been generous in allowing us to use images from their collections—Donald Soeffing, Jean Callan King, and authors Eleanor Fordyce and David Miller—as have many institutions. Photographs from the collections of the Minnesota Historical Society, the Library of Congress, the Museum of the City of New York, the American Life Foundation, the Avery Architectural and Fine Arts Library at Columbia University, the Smithsonian Institution, Winterthur Museum, the Rochester (N.Y.) Museum and Science Center, and the Rochester Public Library's Local History Division have complemented illustrations from our own collections and have improved the interplay between text and image that is a keystone of Strong Museum publications. We are grateful for this cooperation.

H. J. Swinney Intern Lisa Tolbert helped out in the tedious process of last-minute fact checking before the manuscript went into galleys and listened patiently to my frequent tirades, never directed at her, about fidelity to the source. I am happy that she has seen the manuscript after its meticulous copyediting by Pam Wilkinson at the University of Massachusetts Press, which has demonstrated even greater attention to this goal. I have also to thank Richard Martin at the University of Massachusetts Press for his interest in the Strong Museum, his appreciation of the virtues of this volume and of the museum's aims in this copublication, and his willingness to work with an institution of such tender years.

As director of the Strong Museum interpretation department, Harvey Green has supported me throughout in my effort to establish what we hope is only the first in a series of such jointly published volumes and has managed to help me over some of the rougher roads on the way to this particular one. I am grateful to the authors of all the papers—Clifford Clark, Eleanor Fordyce, John Kasson, David Miller, Dorothy Rainwater, and William Rorabaugh—for their everlasting patience over this long haul as well. But no one knows better what a collaboration this volume has been than Susan Williams and Judy White, and that is because they have had to be involved in every part of it by virtue of their expertise. Susan's insightful work on the history of dining in this country and her ability to write about it gracefully and sensitively has not only greatly enriched my appreciation of the topic, but has also enriched this volume. Judy White, who claims that her major role as interpretation department secretary is to keep us from fighting with each other, is more successful at, and equally necessary for, tying up all the loose ends that show up in a project of this length and complexity. Because I can keep nothing to myself, she has witnessed the bitter and the sweet of this project. She has borne occasional fits of temper, has supported my idiosyncrasies as if she shared them, and has been at least as vigilant about the quality of manuscripts as they leave the museum. I thank all of them, and I hope that in this book they find their compensation.

KATHRYN GROVER
Editor

Dining in America

1 8 5 0 – 1 9 0 0

Introduction

SUSAN R. WILLIAMS

Now stir the fire, and close the shutters fast,
Let fall the curtains, wheel the sofa round,
And while the bubbling and loud-hissing urn
Throws up a steamy column, and the cups
That cheer but not inebriate, wait on each,
So let us welcome peaceful evening in.

HESE words of English poet William Cowper evoke for us a powerful and nostalgic vision of the past—whether real or only imagined. The vision carries with it associations of hearth, home, coziness, warmth, nourishment, security, and contentment, all centered around taking tea at the end of the day, a routine family dining ritual in both nineteenth-century England and the United States. But how do we, as cultural historians, transform these words and images into a structure from which we can approach an understanding of our own past? When coupled with the large body of material remains from nineteenth-century America that have been carefully collected by museums and archives—or inadvertently preserved in attics and barns—these words and images become part of a more signifi-

FIG. 1 *A single artifact, such as this silverplated teapot made about 1867 by Reed and Barton of Taunton, Mass., can be interpreted to provide information about technological developments, cultural values, aesthetics, and social rituals.*

cant body of data. These data, when examined within the context of other historical evidence, can help us reconstruct the cultural values that shaped the people and events of the past. In this volume, scholars from a variety of disciplines use an array of resources—both written and artifactual—to examine the rituals, accoutrements, furnishings, and architectural spaces related to middle-class dining in America between 1850 and 1900.

The diverse perspectives of these essayists can fruitfully be applied to the study of the dining activity as a whole or to the analysis of a single material survival of that phenomenon. The readings of that single object are thereby far richer and more telling. Something as ordinary as a teapot, for example, can enlarge our understanding of the beliefs, customs, fears, and goals of Americans who lived long before us. An elegant silver sphere supported by four lion-masked feet and made functional by the addition of a crisply arched spout and angular handle would have charmed the most particular nineteenth-century housewife, especially if it were graced by a coyly balanced ball finial. No matter that it was made not of "real" silver, but of the recently invented electroplate; on the sideboard in a middle-class dining room, surrounded by matching hot water and coffeepots, sugar bowl, cream pitcher, and waste bowl, its effect was as fine as any sterling silver service Tiffany's could have produced (fig. 2).

This teapot, made by Reed and Barton of Taunton, Massachusetts, and in the collection of the Strong Museum, has both an obvious function and a range of symbolic ones. The fact that it was made of silverplate affects its performance and its meaning. As David Miller's essay in this volume points out, the symbolic importance attached to any given artifact does not necessarily imply improvement in its functional characteristics. Many argued that metal was not a suitable material for brewing tea. The Chinese, who introduced tea as a beverage to the Western world in the seventeenth century, used small porcelain or stoneware teapots. These ceramic materials retained heat

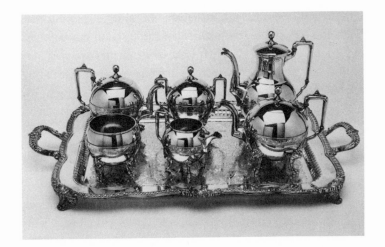

better than metal, and, more important, they were not affected by the acidic content of tea, which tended to develop a metallic taste when brewed in metal pots.

Despite these drawbacks, and despite the fact that teapots made of porcelain or even earthenware could (and did) present an equally impressive display, silver tea utensils were widespread in Victorian America. Silver objects played a critical role in defining a certain level of economic distinction for those who owned and displayed them in their dining rooms. A precious metal, silver had always been an important indication of a family's wealth and social position, but until the discovery in the nineteenth century of the process of electroplating, silver teawares had been out of reach of all but the very rich. The ability to coat base metals with a very thin layer of silver, coupled with the discovery, in 1859, of the Comstock Lode—an enormously rich silver deposit in Nevada—greatly lowered the price of silver and created an entirely new consumer market for silver goods.

Manufacturers of silver teawares such as Reed and Barton quickly adapted this and other new machine technologies to their production. Unlike their predecessors, who had to raise a hollow silver vessel from a flat sheet of silver on a form with a hammer, by 1870 Reed and Barton was able to spin out the body of a teapot on a power-driven lathe, stamp out handles and spouts with newly sophisticated drop presses, roll out bands of elegant trim with rolling machines, and embellish the finished product with "engine-turned" or machine-engraved decoration.

As might be expected, the application of machine technology to the production of silver teapots had an effect on their design. As Dorothy Rainwater's essay substantiates, teapots were fashioned to appeal to the growing body of consumers who favored complicated or whimsical forms, with ornamentation that catered to their interest in ancient Greece and Rome, and Renaissance, baroque, and rococo art. The popular taste for visual complexity was both a by-product of and taskmaster for machine technology. Machines enabled manufacturers to provide increasingly elaborate products with decreasing levels of labor and hand craftsmanship—although by comparison with today's silver production, these teapots had a high degree of skilled labor involved in their fabrication. Because the beverage-dispensing function of a machine-made teapot was little altered from its handmade counterpart, form and design were the two arenas for intense marketing competition among manufacturers. Through the application of machine decoration, a basic teapot (or its fully amplified version, the tea service) could be elaborated in a variety of ways to appeal to diverse tastes, and without necessitating retooling by the manufacturer. E. G. Webster and Brother, a Brooklyn silver manufacturer, for example, advertised in 1880 a "plain" or "plain satin" six-piece tea service for forty-eight dollars. The same tea service could also be had with engraved decoration for an additional eight dollars, or with engraved and hammered decoration (which simulated the handmade look of the planishing hammer) for sixty dollars (fig. 3). Thus, the end product would reflect whatever degree of purchasing power the consumer desired to convey.

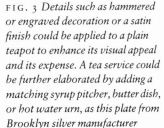

FIG. 3 *Details such as hammered or engraved decoration or a satin finish could be applied to a plain teapot to enhance its visual appeal and its expense. A tea service could be further elaborated by adding a matching syrup pitcher, butter dish, or hot water urn, as this plate from Brooklyn silver manufacturer E. G. Webster's 1880 catalog illustrates.*

Our silverplated, lion-footed, ball-finialed teapot, however, was never intended merely for display. Beyond its beverage-dispensing function, its primary cultural purpose was to enhance the ceremony and ritual that had surrounded the service of tea since Americans first began drinking it in the 1600s. The end, in 1833, of the British East India Company's stranglehold on the production and importation of tea to the West led to a surge in tea-drinking activity (fig. 4). Tea—once a luxury beverage for members of the aristocracy—had traditionally been expensive because of a variety of factors, which began with the high cost of shipping it all the way from China.

.
8
.

Susan R. Williams

FIG. 4 *As this trade card for the Canton Tea Store in Nashua, N.H., attests, a wide assortment of both green and black teas were available by the 1850s, in large cities and smaller towns alike.*

Because of strict controls by the Chinese—who kept as much distance as possible between themselves and Western traders, whom they considered "foreign devils"—the democratizing effect of competition was all but eliminated from the tea market. Once tea arrived in Britain or its colonies, the prices that it commanded were further escalated by the imposition of excise taxes. Finally, in addition to the high cost of tea leaves, the utensils for brewing and drinking tea—generally made either of Chinese (or, by the 1750s, European) porcelain or of silver—were both luxurious and very expensive. The scarcity of these materials connoted wealth, and their faraway origins carried an impression of cosmopolitanism.

The large numbers of teapots—both metal and ceramic—that have survived from the nineteenth century in particular, as well as the multiplicity of written and pictorial accounts of tea drinking, help us to assess the popularity of tea as a beverage and the nature of its consumption. First brought to the West by English and Dutch traders in the seventeenth century, tea became fashionable among the aristocracy in England during the reign of Charles II. By the end of the century, however, the phenomenon had spread to "the *Scholar* and the *Tradesman*," according to J. Ovington, author of *An Essay upon the Nature and Qualities of Tea,* published in 1699.[1] Fewer than fifty

[1] Quoted in Bevis Hillier, *Pottery and Porcelain, 1700–1914* (New York: Meredith Press, 1968), 68.

years later, another British commentator wrote, "Tea . . . is now become so common, that the meanest familys [sic], even of labouring people, particularly in Burroughs, make their morning's Meal of it, . . . and the same Drug supplies all the labouring women with their afternoons' entertainments, . . . at present there are very few Coblers in any of the Burroughs of this Country who do not sit down gravely with their Wives & familys to Tea."[2]

The amount of ceremony with which tea has traditionally been consumed in Western societies stems, no doubt, from its Eastern origins, where taking tea was conducted as an elaborate philosophical ritual, thought to express "conjointly with ethics and religion a whole point of view about man and nature."[3] In nineteenth-century America, the brewing and drinking of tea were frequently enacted with a parallel degree of formality, although not with the same aesthetic and ethical purposes of the Buddhist priests. Sarah Scott, author of *Every-Day Cookery for Every Family* (1868), informed her readers that "the Chinese have a tea-kettle boiling on the table, and put the tea into an ordinary tea-pot, upon which they pour the boiling water, and allow it to stand only a few seconds before it is used. If a second cup is wanted, a fresh infusion is made." She followed this "authentic" version with instructions tailored to American palates: "The most approved method in this country for black tea, is to pour a small quantity of boiling water on the tea; let it stand on a hot stove (not to boil) for twenty minutes, then put it into the tea-pot intended for the table, and fill it up with boiling water. In pouring out black tea into the cup," she added, "always put in the sugar first, then the cream, and the tea last. It alters the flavor entirely to add the sugar or cream afterward."[4]

Tea was an important beverage at two different daily meals—breakfast and "tea." At the breakfast table, tea was brewed, served, and consumed without the formality that typified the latter event, and, in fact, our silverplated teapot would probably have been replaced by a common earthenware model

[2] Quoted from letter by Duncan Forbes, Lord President of the Session to Lord Tweedale, January 1743, in Hillier, *Pottery and Porcelain*, 68, 77.

[3] See Okakura Kakuzo, *The Book of Tea* (New York: Fox, Duffield and Co., 1906), 4.

[4] Quoted in Susan Williams, *Savory Suppers and Fashionable Feasts: Dining in Victorian America* (New York: Pantheon Books and the Strong Museum, 1985), 207.

Susan R. Williams

FIG. 5 *Teapots made of less expensive materials, such as the molded earthenware of this example, would have been used in the kitchen or for informal family meals, especially breakfast. The teapot was decorated with the biblical scene of Rebekah at the well.*

[5] Mrs. M. L. Rayne, *Gems of Deportment* (Detroit: Tyler and Co., 1882), 257. For an extensive survey of the social rituals that surrounded tea drinking in eighteenth-century America, see Rodris Roth, "Tea Drinking in 18th-Century America: Its Etiquette and Equipage," *Contributions from the Museum of History and Technology*, Paper 14, United States National Museum Bulletin 225 (Washington, D.C.: Smithsonian Institution, 1961), 61–91. Further insight into the nature of social relationships between women in the nineteenth century can be gleaned from Carroll Smith-Rosenberg's provocative article,

at the breakfast table (fig. 5). By contrast, tea—which might have been anything from a simple cup of tea, unaccompanied by food, to a family supper, to a full-blown tea party—was generally an important social occasion for all participants, and would have welcomed, if not required, the elegance of a silver or silverplated teapot. By extending this gesture of hospitality, women in particular were provided a vehicle for getting better acquainted with one another. Then as now, these late afternoon events were probably characterized by gossip—speculation, personal or sensational in nature, about people who were not present—the exchange of news about family and friends, and, most likely, the sharing of more intimate details of daily lives. In 1882 etiquette writer M. L. Rayne described teas as lasting "about two hours . . . which time is usually spent in chatting, eating, and exchanging social ideas." Teas were one of the most important forms of social activity for women and helped counteract the isolation of the strictly defined confines of the "woman's sphere" in nineteenth-century America (fig. 6).[5]

Teas were not always events for women only, however, and tea parties were a popular form of heterosexual social activity as well. These events provided a structured and acceptable environment where flirtations, courtship, and male-female friendships could flourish.

As John Kasson points out about the formal dinner, social expectations of "refined" behavior were reinforced by codes of conduct. Such codes also governed the service and consumption of food and drink at tea parties. The rituals that surrounded the service of tea were carefully delineated in etiquette books, cookbooks, and household manuals. American domestic advisers, for example, continually assured their nineteenth-century readers that afternoon teas were supposed to be less formal than dinners or evening parties. The *Cosmopolitan Cook and Recipe Book* claimed in 1888 that tea time was "charming when contrasted with the anxieties, formality and etiquette of the dinner table," but the event still required the

hostess and the guest to discern and tread the fine line between behavior too formal on the one hand and too informal on the other.[6]

Hostesses were to send invitations, either engraved or hand-written, on stationery that was folded into a square shape, and worded according to the specific conventions of the etiquette arbiters. The wise hostess would set her tea table exactly as Catharine Beecher had diagrammed and described it in her popular and much-reprinted *Domestic Receipt Book* of 1842—with a small plate, a knife, a doily or napkin, and a cup plate at each setting, and all teawares arranged prettily on the "waiter," or tea tray (fig. 7).[7]

Guests at an afternoon tea followed explicit rules from the moment they entered the house. They were to "meet informally," Agnes Morton advised in her 1894 volume *Etiquette*, "chatting for a while over a sociable cup of tea, each group giving place to others, none crowding, all at ease, every one the recipient of a gracious welcome from the hostess. . . ." One was to talk to relative strangers "in a chatty, agreeable way," but not to introduce oneself; one was to stay no longer than

FIG. 6 *This stereoview, published by Strohmeyer and Wyman of New York City in 1897 and entitled "Gossip—at every sip a reputation dies," provides a humorous commentary on the role teas played in providing social contact for women in the nineteenth century.*

"The Female World of Love and Ritual: Relations between Women in Nineteenth-Century America," in *The American Family in Social-Historical Perspective*, ed. Michael Gordon (New York: St. Martin's Press, 1978), 334–59.

6 *The Cosmopolitan Cook and Recipe Book*, 3rd ed. (Buffalo: Dingens Brothers, 1888), 12.

7 Catharine E. Beecher, *Miss Beecher's Domestic Receipt Book: Designed as a Supplement to Her Treatise on Domestic Economy*, 3rd ed. (New York: Harper and Brothers, 1858), 244.

Susan R. Williams

FIG. 7 *The rules of etiquette, as
well as the desire to create a scene of
harmony and beauty, governed the
ways that women set their tea
tables, even for an intimate tea in
"My Lady's Chamber," published
in Clarence Cook's* House Beautiful
in 1878.

thirty to forty-five minutes, even though teas generally took
place over two hours' time; one was assured that it was not
vulgar to say "I am taking tea," instead of "I am drinking tea."
Guests were not to dress more formally than they might for
luncheons. Yet, as Mrs. Rayne cautioned, "It is not compli-
mentary to the hostess to drop in with an apology for wearing

a shopping toilet, as if her invitation had been a second thought. Elegant evening toilets are not expected, and would not indicate good taste in the wearer."[8]

Even the simple act of drinking tea was rigidly prescribed, as Marion Harland made clear in her 1883 book *The Cottage Kitchen:* "Tea and coffee must be drunk noiselessly, not sucked, from the side of the cup, leaving the spoon in the saucer, and the cup be held by the handle. I have sat at table with a ponderous D.D., LL.D., and F.F.A., who made me tremble for the dainty china by grasping the cup with his whole hand, the thumb overlapping the brim. . . ." Like teawares themselves, the food served with tea was to be light and graceful: "very thin slices of bread and butter, or wafers, or similar trifles," Agnes Morton suggested.[9] Recipes for tea cakes, waffles and muffins, preserved fruits, biscuits, and other delicacies recommended for the tea table abound in nineteenth-century cookbooks, including the American-written ones that Eleanor Fordyce describes in her essay in this volume. For a more elaborate "high tea" or tea party, some advisers suggested chicken, either broiled or in croquettes, partridges, cold meats cut from a roast, or oysters. But here again, the boundary between propriety and gaffe could easily, even unwittingly, be crossed: as Agnes Morton candidly observed, "The gradations by which the frugal tea passes into the superabundant supper are not easily classified."[10] As David Miller's essay generally attests, the social necessity for a well-furnished tea table required that women also expand their horizons in the kitchen, acquiring a wide range of new cooking skills, as well as the tools that made fashionable and visually impressive "dainties" possible to achieve.

Tea drinking also required an appropriately furnished architectural space, replete with tea table and chairs, a sideboard to display the silver tea implements when not in use, as well as pleasingly decorated walls, windows, and floor. As Clifford Clark has observed, nineteenth-century America demonstrated a popular faith in the power of environment to shape character.

[8] Agnes H. Morton, *Etiquette: An Answer to the Riddle, When? Where? How?* (Philadelphia: Penn Publishing Co., 1894), 67–69; Mrs. H. O. Ward, *Sensible Etiquette of the Best Society* (Philadelphia: Porter and Coates, 1878), 130; Rayne, *Gems of Deportment,* 256–257.

[9] Marion Harland, *The Cottage Kitchen: A Collection of Practical and Inexpensive Receipts* (New York: Charles Scribner's Sons, 1883), 100; Morton, *Etiquette,* 68.

[10] Morton, *Etiquette,* 68.

This belief assured the teapot a place, more or less permanent, in a clearly defined setting. The role that women played in the creation and maintenance of this setting became critically important during the later 1800s, as they shifted from being the major producers of goods for their family's consumption—particularly in the areas of food and textiles—to being consumers of goods now produced outside the home. It was a woman's job to select and integrate those segments of the outside world into her home in such a way as to enrich the entire family by her artistry and her properly moderate tastes.

The very act of pouring a cup of tea from the teapot into a dainty porcelain cup carried with it implications about the political attitudes of both pourer and drinker. As William Rorabaugh's essay makes clear, the consumption of certain beverages—tea, mineral water, and lemonade among them—embodied by inference a whole array of middle-class values about alcohol, religion, patriotism, and social exclusionism. Recall Cowper's description of teas and cups as materials "that cheer but not inebriate."

Just as a multiplicity of meanings can be read out of the teapot, the papers in this volume exemplify the diverse approaches that the Strong Museum takes to the study and interpretation of life in the American middle class during the years 1820 and 1940. Its extensive collections include artifacts related to work, play, social rituals, ceremonies, housing, clothing, feeding, and caring for families and individuals. These artifacts, when viewed collectively, can tell us much about the values, aspirations, superstitions, and traditions that shaped middle-class life in Victorian America.

The material remains that confront historians and curators sometimes challenge current interpretations and presumed meanings. If ceramic teapots brewed better tea, for example, why were silver teapots so prevalent in American homes? The contradictions and ambiguities that cloud our understanding of the cultural meaning of a single artifact such as a silverplated teapot—or of an entire routine, ritualized social event such as dining—can begin to be resolved by synthesizing the findings of several existing scholarly sources not commonly consulted by students of the American past. Anthropologists Mary Douglas, George Armelagos, and Peter Farb have written about foodways and the structure and meaning of meals as well as of specific types of foods. This literature provides a model historians might use to plumb the deeper meaning of the rituals of the Victorian dinner table. The work of Louise Belden of the Winterthur Museum and Caroline Sloat of Old Sturbridge Village, along with several museum exhibitions on "special occasion" and tavern food, have added to the body of knowledge about foodways; still, little attention has been paid to the food traditions of the Victorian American middle class. Swiss sociologist Norbert Elias has written extensively on the rise of etiquette as a social dynamic, and historian Karen Haltunnen has examined behavioral codes in Victorian America, although her work does not specifically focus on behavior in the dining room. Historians Susan Strasser, Ruth Schwartz Cowan, Dolores Hayden, and Harvey Green have explored changes that took place in the nineteenth-century domestic sphere as American women sought to develop new political and ideological, as well as practical, strategies for feeding, clothing, housing, and spiritually nourishing their families. Gwendolyn Wright's work on American domestic architecture provides an added dimension to our investigation of the dedication and elaboration of a specific space for dining in the American home. Much useful work has been done as well by those who focus specifically on artifacts used for food service and food preparation, cataloging changes in the forms, designs, makers, and materials that characterize objects destined for the dining room. This approach, which some dismiss as "antiquarianism," provides researchers with a great deal of primary data without which informed and precise cultural interpretation is impossible.

Although all these studies touch upon aspects of dining in one way or another, none alone provides a comprehensive view of the meaning and significance of dining in American life. In an attempt to begin, and to encourage, the development of this broader picture, in April 1985 the Strong Museum sponsored a two-day symposium on American dining. The goal of the symposium, and of this publication of essays based upon its papers, was to look at the issues and ideas surrounding the Victorian dining room and its rituals from several different vantage points, with the hope of providing a framework through which to understand better social behavior, architecture, diet, and dining habits of middle-class Americans generally in the period between 1850 and 1900. Six leading scholars approached the topic of dining in Victorian America from the perspectives of architecture, etiquette, foodways, serving implements, food preparation, and drinking rituals.

Clifford E. Clark, M.A. and A. D. Hulings Professor of American Studies at Carlton College in Northfield, Minnesota, was invited to participate in this symposium primarily on the basis of his seminal article "Domestic Architecture as an Index to Social History," which has helped shape much thinking about the relationships between domestic architecture, family life, and material culture. His symposium paper, "The Vision of the Model Dining Room: Plan Book Dreams and Middle-Class Realities," analyzed the massive change that took place during the nineteenth century in ideas about the home and the symbolic position of the dining room within it. Using architects' and builders' house plan books and etiquette manuals, Clark investigated how the home was promoted, and how this "advice literature" appears to have affected the way middle-class Americans viewed their homes and furnished them. Earlier seen as a "protected retreat from urban dangers," home was newly promoted after about 1850 as a "vehicle for enhancing self-development and creative expression." Clark's essay expands upon how this shift in perspective changed in turn the artistic and social standards of the home. Using photographs and letters, Clark's essay also examines an issue that has long puzzled students of the nineteenth century: how did "advice literature," one of the most abundant forms of historical evidence available from this period, really affect "middle-class tastes and dining-room experiences"?

Published sections of John F. Kasson's forthcoming book *Civility and Rudeness: Manners in Nineteenth-Century Urban America* made him a natural choice to contribute to the symposium on the topic of table manners. Professor of history and adjunct professor of American studies at the University of North Carolina at Chapel Hill, Kasson draws upon the methodologies of both cultural history and cultural anthropology. His paper, "Rituals of Dining: Table Manners in Victorian America," analyzed dining etiquette as ritual mediation "among ambiguous and frequently contending realms of value." Although table manners were increasingly emphasized and refined in Western civilization from the sixteenth century, they achieved particular importance in late nineteenth-century America, where the "democratization of gentility" became critical to the establishment of order and authority in a restless, mobile, urbanizing, and industrializing democracy. Indeed, Kasson argues, etiquette writers and other "apostles of civility" saw discipline of the appetites and "the manifold gestures expressing them" as part of this larger issue. "Nowhere else," Kasson points out, "were etiquette books so popular as in the United States," and in the last half of the nineteenth century, a major share of their authors' attention was devoted to table manners. In his essay, Kasson describes the recommendations of advice literature on "the supreme test of refinement," the formal dinner. In late nineteenth-century American society, when economic competition was the most virulent it had ever been, dining rituals kept these struggles from permeating the private spheres of friendship and family, and from subverting social distinction.

David W. Miller, a Massachusetts-based kitchenware consultant and researcher, departed from the realm of manners and etiquette for the realm of food itself in his symposium paper, "Technology and the Ideal: American Kitchens and

Kitchen Equipment between 1850 and 1900." His initial research on copper food molds for Revere Copper and Brass has led to a generalized expertise in technological innovations that changed the structure and output of American kitchens during the second half of the nineteenth century. Chief among these was the national mechanization of production, which changed not only the kitchen as a physical space but also the way Americans began to think about the room in which food was prepared and the objects and equipment within that room. Miller's expanded essay in this volume focuses closely on how the "new sensibility" of mechanization affected the design and manufacture of the food mold in America, and the consequences of those decisions on the actual ability of the mold to produce a successful molded dessert. The essay also describes the evolution of domestic science—the culinary school movement, public education, and college curricula—and how kitchenware manufacturers responded selectively to its vision of the ideal kitchen.

Eleanor T. Fordyce brought a dietitian's insight as well as a highly specific collector's knowledge of American cookbooks to her topic, "Cookbooks of the 1800s: American Authored and American Published." Since 1954 Fordyce has assembled a body of almost 700 cookbooks—all written or published in this country—which she uses to trace the history and changes in nineteenth-century American cookery.

Cookbooks, she notes, have often gone beyond the mere presentation of instructions for preparing dishes; they have also consistently reflected historic foodways, general customs, and ways of thinking. The cookbook was frequently "the woman's only book," in an age when little professional assistance or advice was available and population mobility weakened the intergenerational network of the family as a source of instruction. Using numerous excerpts from cookbooks, Fordyce's essay documents their response to a growing sense of national and regional identity, to the century's interest in increasing precision in measurement, and to the influence of the cooking school movement and "domestic science."

Dorothy Rainwater is well known to collectors, curators, and scholars of nineteenth-century American silver. She is the author of six books on that topic, as well as of numerous articles published in collectors' magazines, trade journals, educational journals, and newspapers. Rainwater has done extensive research in trade catalogs, advertising literature, and other commercial sources, analyzing marketing trends and changing fashion in silver tablewares, as well as recording the identifying trademarks used by hundreds of different manufacturers. Her symposium paper, "American Dining Room Silver," examined the forms and functions of Victorian dining room silver from the point of view, widely held by middle-class Americans in the last fifty years of the nineteenth century, that Victorians "never showed themselves to better advantage than in acquitting themselves well in serving their guests." Her talk traced the rise of silver as "the chief status symbol of the Victorian era." Rainwater's essay in this volume describes the traditional use of gold and silver to express power and fortune, the increasing demand for ornamentation in silver patterns, and the ability of the machine stamping process to satisfy this desire.

Rainwater describes tablewares of special importance to American Victorians—the revolving silver condiment caster, the cake basket and the excessive elaboration of its design in the 1870s and 1880s, and the development and later profusion of napkin rings. She also discusses how available technology in food processing influenced tableware forms such as the circular butter dish. Still, many forms of tablewares were so greatly overburdened with ornamentation that their form was obscured and their function hampered.

William J. Rorabaugh, associate professor in the Department of History at the University of Washington in Seattle and author of *The Alcoholic Republic: An American Tradition* (1979), used census reports, demographic studies, labor histories, church records, and the literature of the temperance reformers in his paper, "Beer, Lemonade, and Propriety in the Gilded Age." His research demonstrates the socioeconomic difference in nineteenth-century drinking patterns. Between the end of the Civil War and the beginning of the twentieth century, Rorabaugh argues, American middle-class drinking habits underwent a profound change: while beer displaced whiskey as the alcoholic beverage of choice, the movement for total abstinence from alcohol grew even stronger. Abstinence became associated with respectability and propriety; American feelings about alcohol became infused with guilt and ambivalence and were complicated by the class and ethnic associations of liquor. Rorabaugh's essay in this volume analyzes the role of middle-class women in the antiliquor crusade. Standing at its core, women took on alcohol as part of a larger attack on a whole range of male-oriented symbols.

Several recurring themes serve as the warp for the overall fabric of these six papers. The most obvious is the character and impact of the middle class in the United States. The second half of the nineteenth century was a period of great social change. For the first time, the middle class emerged as a powerful entity, one that dominated the value structure and patterns of consumption in this country. Middle-class Americans worked hard to elevate themselves socially and to maintain and symbolize that position by emulating the cosmopolitan lifestyles of the elites, adopting social practices and codes of behavior that would at the same time distinguish them from the laboring classes. Yet middle-class Americans also felt it necessary to set themselves apart from the negative characteristics of elites, the tendencies toward indolence and luxury that they perceived great wealth to have wrought. They viewed the constant exercise of self-control and personal and social propriety essential to the preservation of their distinct culture, especially in the face of rapidly increasing population pressure from large numbers of southern and eastern European immigrants. These newcomers brought with them traditions and customs that were perceived by many as a threat to the hegemony of middle-class values, even to its American— precisely Anglo-American—way of life. As Rorabaugh notes, it was immigrants from Germany who introduced new methods of brewing beer; the resulting increase in the popularity and consumption of this intoxicating and inexpensive beverage—particularly among members of the laboring classes— fueled the fires of class struggle within the context of the temperance movement for years to come.

Rorabaugh's paper opens with a detailed analysis of the composition of the middle class, providing a clear picture of its economic structure, consumer power, occupations, ethnicity, and family values—in particular, its emphasis on propriety. As the middle class emerged as a powerful social force, its members looked increasingly toward codified forms of behavior as a means of defining and solidifying their position in a changing society. Temperance was one of those behaviors. Knowledge and display of correct etiquette, as Kasson points out, was another.

Etiquette exemplifies another important defining characteristic of middle-class culture—the conspicuous emulation of the behaviors and tastes of the wealthy. Similarly, Rainwater's essay identifies the acquisition of gold and silver tablewares as traditional indicators of power and wealth. These associations were widely perceived by the middle class, which by the middle of the nineteenth century was able to express its achievement of respectable status and affluence by acquiring silver or its less expensive facsimile, silverplate. Clark's analysis of architectural plan books identifies the dining room—once a luxury found only in homes of the very wealthy—"as the hallmark of the achievement of middle-class respectability." He goes on to state that "by the 1880s, evidence from the plan books indicates that the more elaborate mealtime rituals formerly limited to the wealthy had started to become more typical, on a smaller scale, in middle-class houses." And Miller also develops the concept of status emulation in his discussion of the social importance of the copper food mold: "For Victorians, the mold 'spoke of habits and tastes,' both literal and cultural. It supplied both decorative character to the table and implications about one's civilized habits and social position."

Another recurring theme is the increasing cultural valuation of specialization during the second half of the nineteenth century. Eating behavior became more involved and complex, architectural spaces dedicated specifically to cooking and dining began to appear in the home, and a wide range of functionally specific implements were produced for preparing, serving, and eating foods.

A nineteenth-century concern with elaboration is also apparent in the preoccupation with style and ornament in tablewares, as well as in both spatial and behavioral terms. Behavior at the dining table became more ceremonial, and decoration of the dining space began to reflect an emphasis on the home-maker's "self-development and creative expression," another middle-class hallmark of the latter nineteenth century. Artistically decorated dining rooms and elegantly prepared and presented meals could express social competence and individual power. Miller's discussion of changing methods of food preparation brings into focus the tension between social and individual interests in elaboration and display and the functional and economic imperatives of factory production.

The role of middle-class women in the nineteenth-century social structure is another link between several of the essays. Clark indirectly analyzes the changing nature of housework in his discussion of the "new interest in artistic creativity" which women expressed "in a wide range of everyday affairs from the decoration of rooms to the preparation of food." Both Miller's and Fordyce's essays reveal dramatic changes in women's roles as housework in general, and cookery specifically, came under professional and scientific scrutiny. In their discussions of the leadership and membership in the temperance movement and of the "material feminist" movement respectively, Rorabaugh and Miller provide further insight into how women responded to nineteenth-century social change.

It is hoped that the constellation of ideas presented in these essays, revolving around the general theme of nineteenth-century dining rituals, will provide a starting point for further inquiry into other and broader questions about the attitudes and values of the Victorian middle class.

Beer, Lemonade, and Propriety in the Gilded Age

W . J . R O R A B A U G H

 hundred years ago American drinking habits indicated social class, and the middle classes of the small towns and large cities of the rapidly industrializing Northeast and Midwest mainly drank nonalcoholic beverages (fig. 1). But before describing middle-class habits in detail, let me define more precisely the middle classes. The middle classes did not include the rich merchants, large-scale landowners, and successful speculators, who constituted the wealthiest tenth of the people owning half the nation's wealth. Nor did the middle classes include household servants, unskilled laborers, factory operatives, or store clerks, who were the poorest half of the people with little or no property. The middle classes were the 40 percent of the people between the wealthiest tenth and the poorest half; they owned about half the wealth.

There was a great deal of variation within the middle classes.

W. H. MURRAY,

MANUFACTURER OF

Lemon and Sarsaparilla Beer,

AND ALL KINDS OF

TEMPERANCE DRINKS,

No. 17 Glasgow Street,   -   Rochester, N. Y.

FIG. 1 *Businessmen in the Gilded Age turned to marketing a number of nonalcoholic beverages, an activity that eventually led to what might be deemed a major American contribution to world civilization —cola-flavored soft drinks. Advertisement, Rochester, N.Y., Directory (1871).*

At the top, with the largest incomes, were professionals such as doctors, lawyers, and ministers. By the 1880s, a few people had entered new professions—accountants, architects, and engineers, for example. The middle classes also included some merchants and storekeepers who owned and operated small businesses. Further down the income scale, but still within the middle classes, were master craftsmen such as carpenters, blacksmiths, and ironmongers, who owned their own businesses, employed others, and made a good living from specialized knowledge of skilled work. Also in the middle classes were middle managers in factories and large stores, and many of the lesser clerks who made these businesses function. At the bottom of the middle classes were a number of skilled craftsmen in highly skilled trades, for example, journeymen machinists or pattern molders who could earn up to ten dollars a day.

In terms of income, the middle classes earned between $500 and $2,000 a year. During the 1880s, an unskilled laborer earned about $250 a year, which was not enough to support a family. A family of four required $400 to $600 to live above the poverty level. Thus, a married unskilled laborer with children had to send his wife and children into factories and stores to supplement his own meager income. Although the children of the poor were attending school longer than their parents had, they often missed the kind of education necessary for entry into the ranks of the middle classes.

A man who earned $500 a year was middle class because he could support a family without having a wife or children who worked. But with $500 a year, a family was only barely middle class. There would be no savings, no margin for the purchase of luxuries, and no chance to buy a house. What made such a family middle class was its devotion to propriety and its determination to see that the children who did not have to work received educations that would enable them to earn good wages. By contrast, a middle-class family with an income of $2,000 a year could save money, eventually buy a house, and maintain at least one live-in servant. Probably half of all middle-class families had one servant, often an Irish kitchen maid. If a man earned more than $2,000 a year, he could afford more than one servant and consider himself rich.

In the 1880s, the middle classes in the small towns and large cities of the Northeast and Midwest were overwhelmingly descended from families who had been in the United States for generations. Perhaps three-quarters of the middle classes could trace their ancestry back to the time of the American Revolution. In a country that was increasingly populated either by immigrants or by second-generation children of immigrants, the old-stock ancestry of the middle classes stood out. They were most likely of English, Scots, or Scots-Irish descent, unless they lived in Pennsylvania, where they might claim German ancestry, or in New York, where the Dutch had settled. In any case, middle-class Americans, like their ancestors, were overwhelmingly Protestant. This fact caused little comment, because from colonial times America had been a Protestant country. But by the 1880s, a vast change was underway. Among the poorest half of the people in the small towns and large cities of the Northeast and Midwest, probably three-quarters were immigrants or the children of immigrants. Most of these immigrants were Irish, German, or English—particularly Irish and German (fig. 2). In addition, by the 1880s a few Italians and eastern European Jews had begun to arrive. Most

Beer, Lemonade, and Propriety

FIG. 2 *In this political cartoon, Uncle Sam warns immigrants to give up ties to their homelands and become Americans. The interest of Germans in beer is symbolized by St. Gambrinus—the mythical king of Flanders, inventor of beer, and Germany's patron saint of drinking. "Reform Is Necessary in the Foreign Line," Thomas Nast, cover engraving of* Harper's Weekly *(14 April 1877).*

¹ These paragraphs are drawn both from my own examination of the manuscript census for 1880 and from numerous community studies. For example, see Merle Curti, with assistance of Robert Daniel and others, *The Making of an American Community: A Case Study of Democracy in a Frontier County* (Stanford: Stanford University Press, 1959); Alan Dawley, *Class and Community: The Industrial Revolution in Lynn* (Cambridge: Harvard University Press, 1976); Clyde Griffen and Sally Griffen, *Natives and Newcomers: The Ordering of Opportunity in Mid-Nineteenth-Century Poughkeepsie* (Cambridge: Harvard University Press, 1978); Hartmut Keil and John B. Jentz, eds., *German Workers in Industrial Chicago, 1850–1910: A Comparative Perspective* (DeKalb: Northern Illinois University Press, 1983); Steven J. Ross, *Workers on the Edge: Work, Leisure and Politics in Industrializing Cincinnati, 1788–1890* (New York: Columbia

of the immigrants were Catholic or Jewish. Thus, by the 1880s there was a cleavage between the old-stock, Protestant middle classes and the immigrant working classes. Although the split was along economic lines, it presented a clash of cultural values.¹

One issue that divided working-class and middle-class Amer-

University Press, 1985); Daniel J. Walkowitz, *Worker City, Company Town: Iron and Cotton Worker Protest in Troy and Cohoes, New York, 1855–1884* (Urbana: University of Illinois Press, 1978); John H. Cordulack, "The Artisan Confronts the Machine Age: Bureau County, Illinois, 1850–1880" (Ph.D. diss., University of Illinois, Urbana, 1975); Paul B. Hensley, "An Eighteenth-Century World Not Quite Lost: The Social and Economic Structure of a Northern New York Town, 1810–1880" (Ph.D. diss., College of William and Mary, Williamsburg, 1979). The best study of education is Lawrence A. Cremin, *American Education: The National Experience, 1783–1876* (New York: Harper and Row, 1980).

[2] In general, see W. J. Rorabaugh, *The Alcoholic Republic* (New York: Oxford University Press, 1979), 185–222; Ian R. Tyrrell, *Sobering Up: From Temperance to Prohibition in Antebellum America, 1800–1860* (Westport, Conn.: Greenwood Press, 1979). See the suggestive although methodologically flawed study by George G. Wittet, "Concerned Citizens: The Prohibitionists of 1883 Ohio," in *Alcohol, Reform and Society: The Liquor Issue in Social Context*, ed. Jack S.

icans—and particularly antagonized the middle classes—was the consumption of alcoholic beverages. After 1825, old-stock Protestants, under the influence of evangelical religion, had turned increasingly against liquor. Traditionally, Americans had drunk mostly whiskey and other hard liquor, and as old-stock attitudes had changed, consumption of those beverages declined (fig. 3). At the same time, immigrants brought their own drinking habits to the country, and rising immigrant consumption partially offset declining old-stock consumption. One important change, as shown in table 1, was the rise in consumption of beer.[2]

TABLE I   Alcoholic beverage consumption per capita of total population, in U.S. gallons

	Spirits		Wine		Beer		
	Gallons	% Absolute Alcohol	Gallons	% Absolute Alcohol	Gallons	% Absolute Alcohol	Total Absolute Alcohol
1825	5.0	2.2	.2	<.05	–	–	3.7*
1840	3.1	1.4	.3	.1	1.3	.1	1.8*
1855	2.2	1.0	.2	<.05	2.7	.1	1.1
1870	1.9	.9	.3	.1	5.2	.3	1.3
1885	1.4	.6	.5	.1	11.4	.6	1.3
1900	1.2	.5	.4	.1	15.5	.8	1.4

*Figures for 1825 and 1840 include hard cider
SOURCE: W. J. Rorabaugh, *The Alcoholic Republic* (New York: Oxford University Press, 1979), 232.

Traditionally, Americans had drunk little beer; as late as 1840, consumption was barely above a gallon per person. Low consumption was related to poor quality; English-style brewers had discovered that their brewing techniques did not work well in the humid American climate. (It was a technical problem: the English brewed with a top-floating yeast, and in the United States the yeast picked up wild yeasts in the air that turned the beer bitter.) During the 1840s and 1850s, German

FIG. 3 *American glass manufac-turers produced a variety of flasks, bottles, and canteens which were designed and had long been used to carry spiritous liquors. Clockwise from top: the aqua-colored glass flask decorated with scrolled ribs, fleur-de-lis, and petaled flowers was made late in the 1800s by Bakewell, Page and Bakewell of Pittsburgh; the oyster-shaped whiskey bottle to its right was made in 1891 by William T. Murphy of New York City; the amber-colored bottle in the shape of a pistol was made by an unidentified American manu-facturer; and the clear glass canteen with a label honoring Admiral Dewey, hero of the Spanish-American War of 1898, is also American but of unidentified manufacture.*

immigrants arrived with new brewing methods. They made lager beer, which was brewed with a heavy, sinking yeast that was not exposed to the air and hence yielded a better brew. By the 1850s, beer drinking had begun to catch on throughout the country; indeed, the *New York Times* became alarmed at the growth of this immigrant industry (fig. 4). German immigrants not only brewed but also opened beer gardens in the suburbs of large cities, and the gardens attracted both immigrants and native-born Americans. Then came the Civil War, and the Union Army furnished troops with beer rations—in place of the traditional and more intoxicating rum rations. In 1862 the federal government began to tax alcoholic beverages. Distillers paid two dollars per gallon, but brewers got a more favorable rate—three cents a gallon—because they were enthusiastic supporters of the war. Tax discrimination helped drive drink-ers from expensive whiskey to cheap beer, and annual per

Blocker, Jr. (Westport, Conn.: Greenwood Press, 1979), 111–47. For a provocative theoretical stance, see Joseph R. Gusfield, *Symbolic Crusade: Status Politics and the American Temperance Movement* (Urbana: University of Illinois Press, 1963).

W. J. Rorabaugh

FIG. 4 *German immigrants were given credit (or blame) for introducing beer to Americans. In this enameled porcelain pitcher, made in Trenton, N.J., around 1876, King Gambrinus stands with a keg of beer at his feet and holds a stein in his hand as he introduces the beverage to Uncle Sam.*

[3] On brewing, see Stanley Baron, *Brewed in America: A History of Beer and Ale in the United States* (Boston: Little, Brown and Co., 1962), esp. 185, 211–36, 257–59; August F. Fehlandt, *A Century of Drink Reform in the United States* (Cincinnati: Jennings and Graham, 1904), 157, 159; Rorabaugh, *Alcoholic Republic*, 106–10, 232.

capita consumption of beer more than doubled between 1870 and 1885. Meanwhile, hard liquor consumption declined, and wine consumption remained negligible. By 1890, half the alcohol consumed in the United States was in the form of beer (fig. 5). Prospering breweries included those founded by Busch, Schlitz, Blatz, and Miller (a son-in-law of the founder of Pabst, originally Müller).[3]

What drove respectable middle-class Americans into a campaign against beer was not only its foreign origin but also its sale in the all-male saloon. In every town and city, saloons were to be found on practically every street corner (fig. 6). In Boston, for example, ninety-five saloons were within two blocks of city hall. Most saloons were under the control of the brewers, who used their economic power to coerce saloonkeepers into one-sided contracts that dictated wholesale prices and prohibited retailers from selling competing brands. Saloonkeepers faced

FIG. 5 *As beer became more popular, the brewing industry increasingly identified its product with American themes. This stein, made in Germany for the American market around 1900, features three scenes from Rochester, N.Y.*

pressure from their suppliers to increase sales, while competition kept retail prices low and threatened profits. Many retailers found that the only way they could survive financially was to sell to children and teenagers, to violate local ordinances that prohibited sales on Sundays, or to operate gambling parlors and whorehouses in back rooms. To lure customers, the saloons also offered a free lunch. For five cents a customer bought not only a glass of beer but also the right to fill a plate

FIG. 6 *In the late nineteenth century, Batholomay beer and ale could be purchased both at William P. Buckley's café and at the adjacent Kelly Brothers' store. Courtesy Stone Negative Collection, Rochester Museum and Science Center, Rochester, N.Y.*

[4] Perry R. Duis, *The Saloon: Public Drinking in Chicago and Boston, 1880–1920* (Urbana: University of Illinois Press, 1983), 20–45, 188. The classic description is George Ade, *The Old-Time Saloon: Not Wet—Not Dry, Just History* (New York: R. Long and R. R. Smith, 1931). See also Thomas J. Noel, *The City and the Saloon: Denver, 1858–1916* (Lincoln: University of Nebraska Press, 1982); Roy Rosenzweig, *Eight Hours for What We Will: Workers and Leisure in an Industrial City* (New York: Cambridge University Press, 1983).

from free food kept at the bar. Salty items such as pretzels, salted herring, sour pickles, and potato salad were favored; they created thirst and kept up beer sales. Many factory workers went to saloons at noon for beer and free lunches, and many more stopped off at saloons on the way home from work. Some staggered out of saloons drunk, and others became involved in saloon brawls.[4]

Although the middle classes saw saloons as dens of vice, immigrant working men clung to their saloons and refused to abandon them. The middle classes did not understand that in a country where they controlled or operated virtually every important institution, the only truly working-class institution (save the Catholic church) was the saloon (fig. 7). If an immigrant needed a job, he did not have rich relatives and old family ties to help him secure one; instead, he sought help from his saloonkeeper, who functioned as a job placement officer. An immigrant might solicit a job from a foreman by buying the man a drink. If an immigrant needed a loan, he did not dare go to a bank or try to borrow from relatives; instead, he borrowed

FIG. 7 *At the turn of the century, a man could buy a drink at the Francis Doud Saloon, 79 Front Street, Rochester, N.Y. Note the wooden floor, simple furniture, plain ceiling, brass spittoons, and elegant bar behind which was kept the supply of enticing liquors. Courtesy Rochester (N.Y.) Public Library, Local History Division.*

money from the saloonkeeper, who was both moneylender and pawnbroker. Or the immigrant might meet a friend in a saloon in order to obtain money to meet an emergency. If an immigrant wanted to participate in politics, it was the saloonkeeper who arranged for his vote, and the voter could expect to be rewarded with a drink. Indeed, saloons were the base for the emerging immigrant political machines. It was the working class's autonomy and power expressed in the saloon that drove the middle classes into opposition to drinking houses.[5]

The middle-class attack on saloons was determined—even violent and hysterical (fig. 8). One middle-class attorney described a saloon this way: "As we approach its door, we hear the ear-torturing music of an asthmatic Dutch organ mingled with the beer-soiled notes of the 'Faderland.'" The attorney smelled stale beer, "whose nastiness of composition" was "only rivaled by its taste." The pretzels at the free lunch were "salt as the ocean's brine." Worst of all, at least to this anti-German observer, was Limburger cheese. "If all the vile odors from the public sewers were mingled with those of Chicago's

[5] Duis, *Saloon,* 114–42. An excellent novel describing immigrant saloons is Thomas Bell, *Out of This Furnace* (Boston: Little, Brown and Co., 1941), esp. 29, 43, 45, 47, 67–68, 92–93, 157, 161, 187–89. For a defense of saloons see William L. Riordon, *Plunkitt of Tammany Hall: A Series of Very Plain Talks on Very Practical Politics* (New York: Dutton, 1963).

FIG. 8 *Middle-class opponents of alcohol tended to portray the substance in exaggerated ways. In this drawing, liquor has assumed the shape of an idol worthy of a Christian's attack. "King Alcohol,"* engraving in James Shaw, History of the Great Temperance Reforms of the Nineteenth Century *(Cincinnati, 1875). Courtesy Wheaton College Library.*

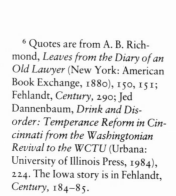

[6] Quotes are from A. B. Richmond, *Leaves from the Diary of an Old Lawyer* (New York: American Book Exchange, 1880), 150, 151; Fehlandt, *Century*, 290; Jed Dannenbaum, *Drink and Disorder: Temperance Reform in Cincinnati from the Washingtonian Revival to the WCTU* (Urbana: University of Illinois Press, 1984), 224. The Iowa story is in Fehlandt, *Century*, 184–85.

fragrant river and glue factories; if all these could be combined in one stupendous, overwhelming, sickening stench," he wrote, "it would be sweet as the ottar of roses compared with that cheese." Or, as another middle-class spokesman put it, German culture had been ruined by "its beer jokes, its beer literature, and its beer conversation." When a group of female antiliquor protesters tried to close down a German beer garden, the proprietor resisted. His words were recorded (satirically) in an antiliquor newspaper: "Go vay, vimmins, go home; shtay at home, and tend to your papies. . . ." These clashes between old-stock, dry Protestants and immigrant, wet Catholics sometimes led to violence. In 1886 a Methodist minister in Sioux City, Iowa, was assassinated while driving his team through a proliquor crowd. The minister had taken a leading role in enforcing a local prohibition ordinance, and at a meeting of the saloonkeepers' association one brewer had offered money for the minister's death. The brewer was brought to trial but acquitted, and the jury afterward adjourned to a photo studio where they sat for a photograph with the brewer in the center of the picture.[6]

By the 1880s, in contrast with beer-drinking immigrants,

FIG. 9 *Middle-class fascination with exotic foods stimulated imports, among them citrus fruits and bananas.* Harper's Weekly *recorded the activity in a June 1870 issue in "Landing Tropical Fruits at Burling Slip, New York," engraved after a drawing by A. R. Ward.*

middle-class Americans increasingly enjoyed a higher standard of living that enabled them to reshape their diet with new and previously exotic foods. Bananas, which had been exhibited at Philadelphia in 1876, became popular; so did oranges and tangerines. By the 1880s, pineapples sold in northern markets for as little as twenty-five cents apiece (fig. 9). In time, railroads brought California citrus; at the World's Columbian Exposition in Chicago in 1893, California displayed a tower of fresh oranges surrounded by a sea of lemons. These new foods both changed eating habits and led to new patterns of beverage consumption. For the first time, fruit-flavored soft drinks made with soda water became popular. Not only could delicious nonalcoholic drinks be made simply and easily from pineapples, oranges, and lemons, but the introduction of so many new foods led middle-class Americans to experiment with beverages other than the old-fashioned liquor kept on the sideboard. Alcohol's greatest claim to virtue had come from its ties to the past, to ritual, and to tradition. What encouraged the middle classes to dispense with alcohol, in addition to the

FIG. 10 *Mrs. Lucy Webb Hayes,*
wife of President Rutherford
Birchard Hayes, was an indefati-
gable antiliquor reformer. Her
enthusiasm may have cost her
husband renomination to the presi-
dency. Engraving in Frances E.
Willard, Woman and Temperance
(Hartford, Conn., 1883).

tenets of evangelical religion, was rising affluence, an atmosphere of experimentation, and easy access to previously exotic
foods and beverages.[7]

One experimenter was Lucy Hayes, wife of President
Rutherford B. Hayes (fig. 10). Mrs. Hayes was both a devout
Methodist and a teetotaler, and after her husband became
president in 1877, she declared that no alcoholic beverages
would be served in the White House. Her policy was in sharp
contrast with that of the Grant administration, which had
come to an end with a reputation for hard drinking amid a
whiskey-tax scandal. Thirsty politicians did not like Lucy
Hayes's policy, and they began to ridicule the first lady.

[7] Richard J. Hooker, *Food and*
Drink in America: A History
(Indianapolis: Bobbs-Merrill,
1981), 232–33, 272–78.

"Lemonade Lucy" wore the cause as a badge of honor, although she did herself no good when she sat for an ostentatious portrait painted under the sponsorship of the Woman's Christian Temperance Union. While Lucy Hayes established proper middle-class behavior at the White House, the politicians plotted their revenge: in 1880, Hayes was denied renomination, at least in part due to controversy about his wife's temperance activities. At that time neither Republicans nor Democrats wished to be identified too closely with the antiliquor movement, because the cause threatened party harmony.[8]

Lucy Hayes was from Ohio, where middle-class women had begun to crusade against alcohol and saloons in 1873. Late that year, a traveling lecturer had casually suggested to a group of women in Hillsboro, Ohio, that they could close that small town's saloons by organizing pray-ins. The day after the lecture, fifty women met to plan their campaign to rid the town of the hated saloons. Perhaps because these middle-class women envisioned themselves as participants in a "holy war," they called themselves Crusaders; their leader was Eliza Thompson, the daughter of a governor, wife of a judge, and mother of an alcoholic minister—a quintessentially upper-middle-class woman. (It is worth noting that before accepting the chairmanship of the group, Mrs. Thompson asked for and received her husband's consent.) Every day these women visited a different saloon in Hillsboro and asked the merchant to stop selling liquor (fig. 11). If their request was refused, the Crusaders sat down and began to pray aloud and sing religious songs. The saloonkeepers were astonished that the women were so bold as to enter the all-male world of the saloon. The crusade had its intended effect, for within a few weeks the number of liquor dealers in Hillsboro declined from thirteen to four. Other towns took up the crusade, the *New York Tribune* sent a reporter to cover the movement, and within a year the crusade had spread to 912 towns and cities in thirty-one states.[9]

At first saloonkeepers did not know how to respond to the

[8] Emily A. Geer, *First Lady: The Life of Lucy Webb Hayes* (Kent, Ohio: Kent State University Press, 1984), esp. 147–55, 217–18, 220–24. The best survey of the late nineteenth-century temperance movement remains Daniel Dorchester, *The Liquor Problem in All Ages* (Cincinnati: Walden and Stowe, 1884).

[9] Ruth Bordin, *Woman and Temperance: The Quest for Power and Liberty, 1873–1900* (Philadelphia: Temple University Press, 1981), esp. 15–20, 22, 31; Dannenbaum, *Drink and Disorder*, 180–82, 212–14. For a detailed analysis, see Charles A. Isetts, "A Social Profile of the Women's Temperance Crusade: Hillsboro, Ohio," in Blocker, *Alcohol, Reform and Society*, 101–10. See also Barbara L. Epstein, *The Politics of Domesticity: Women, Evangelism, and Temperance in Nineteenth-Century America* (Middletown, Conn.: Wesleyan University Press, 1981), 95–100. The newly definitive study is Jack S. Blocker, Jr., *"Give to the Winds Thy Fears": The Women's Temperance Crusade, 1873–1874* (Westport, Conn.: Greenwood Press, 1985).

W. J. Rorabaugh

FIG. 11 *In 1874, the Crusaders invaded saloons, where they prayed, sang, lectured, and wept to persuade customers to give up drink and saloonkeepers to give up the trade. "Lady Crusaders," engraving in James Shaw,* History of the Great Temperance Reforms. *Courtesy Wheaton College Library.*

[10] Bordin, *Woman and Temperance,* 20, 23–24; Dannenbaum, *Drink and Disorder,* 212–26. On women as moral guardians, see Barbara Welter, "The Cult of True Womanhood, 1820–1860," *American Quarterly* 18 (1966): 151–74; Ann Douglas, *The Feminization of American Culture* (New York: Alfred A. Knopf, 1977).

Crusaders. Some tried to reason with the women, but their arguments were met by choruses of "Nearer My God to Thee." Other saloonkeepers quickly locked their doors whenever they spotted groups of women marching down the sidewalks. Some got court injunctions prohibiting sit-ins, but the Crusaders sometimes refused to obey court orders and dared public officials to arrest women engaged in moral protest. Because women were generally considered to be the moral guardians of society, such arrests became exercises in the grotesque. Still other saloonkeepers poured sour beer on the Crusaders. The women developed their own responses to such tactics. In small towns, where public reputation was essential for a successful middle-class life, the Crusaders subjected drinkers to public notice. In Washington Court House, Ohio, for example, women took down the names of all the men who were seen visiting a suburban beer garden; every day, they read the list of names in the middle of the town square (fig. 12).[10]

The tactics that worked in the small towns did not succeed in the larger cities. When the Crusaders marched through German neighborhoods in Dayton, Ohio, they had sausage and beer hurled at them, and the wives of saloonkeepers

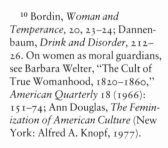

EVER LET LOVE AND TRUTH PREVAIL.

FIG. 12 *In a small town, a saloon-keeper found it difficult to resist the personal pleas of women who were his neighbors and the wives, mothers, and daughters of his customers.* "Pleading with a Saloonist," *engraving in James Shaw,* History of the Great Temperance Reforms. *Courtesy Wheaton College Library.*

screamed obscenities. The prayer bands continued to march, and they agitated for local-option prohibition. Finally, when Dayton voted on the question of making the city dry, the immigrant vote gave the wets a victory. Afterward, Dayton officials used the police to bar the women from marching through the streets. In Cincinnati, the Crusaders confronted an immigrant political machine intimately linked to liquor; twenty-three of forty-eight city councilmen were in the trade. There the Crusaders closed no saloons, were attacked with rotten eggs, and finally were arrested for marching without a parade permit (fig. 13).[11]

Whether these middle-class women had a chance to succeed

[11] Bordin, *Woman and Temperance,* 25; Dannenbaum, *Drink and Disorder,* 217, 218, 222–25.

FIG. 13 *The Cincinnati Crusaders made national headlines
when police arrested forty-three
women for singing and praying in
the streets. "Jewels among Swine,"
cover engraving of* Harper's
Weekly *(13 June 1874).*

or not, they marched in order to establish, in both native and
immigrant eyes, what constituted proper middle-class behavior. Propriety was the real issue, and abstinence from alcohol
was the means by which propriety was established. It was this
dimension of the liquor question that explains why middle-
class women were willing, even eager, to march through immigrant neighborhoods provoking confrontations in large

cities that were hopelessly under the control of liquor-oriented political machines. The crusade was intended to define publicly what constituted proper behavior.[12] Explained one Cincinnati newspaper, "It raises up a public sentiment, zeal, enthusiasm, and influence which unite the community in the cause, and which will make drinking disreputable. In this it seems to us will be its great and permanent effects." The women established that respectable middle-class Americans should not drink alcoholic beverages.[13]

The Crusaders of 1873–74 recognized the need for a permanent organization to promote their cause, and they soon created the Woman's Christian Temperance Union. Under the dynamic and forceful leadership of Frances Willard, in time the WCTU became the most powerful middle-class woman's organization in the United States. Although most middle-class women never joined the WCTU, many were sympathetic to its two main goals—the prohibition of all alcoholic beverages and women's suffrage. To the WCTU, liquor was the source of crime, poverty, wife beating, child abandonment, and political corruption. Every social ill of modern, industrial, urban society was blamed on strong drink. These women believed that the cure for the liquor problem was the legal prohibition of the sale of alcohol. Perhaps some prohibitionists naively believed that antiliquor laws would eliminate the demon rum, but the more politically astute recognized that some liquor always would remain. Reformers, however, hoped that liquor consumption would fall, that the social ills it provoked would be ameliorated, and that those who bought or sold alcohol would be marked as persons deviating from middle-class values. The WCTU also believed that, because women were the moral guardians of society, women's suffrage would uplift and elevate both politics and society. It was this moral dynamic, expressed as a concern for propriety, that provided the basis for the middle-class campaign against alcohol.[14]

In 1885, when the middle classes sat down to Sunday dinner, they did not drink alcoholic beverages. To have drunk whiskey

[12] Dannenbaum, *Drink and Disorder*, 219–20, 222–24; Bordin, *Woman and Temperance*, 32.

[13] Cincinnati *Gazette*, 9 February 1874, quoted in Dannenbaum, *Drink and Disorder*, 222.

[14] Bordin, *Woman and Temperance*, esp. 34–56, 63, 72, 87, 135; Dannenbaum, *Drink and Disorder*, 227–30; George F. Clark, *History of the Temperance Reform in Massachusetts, 1813–1883* (Boston: Clarke and Carruth, 1888), 173–82. In general, see Frances E. Willard, *Glimpses of Fifty Years* (Chicago: H. J. Smith, 1889). I have also profited from reading unpublished work by Ian R. Tyrrell.

FIG. 14 *Wineglasses or water goblets? The answer depended upon the views of the owner. Perhaps one reason for the popularity of cut glass and pressed glass pieces was that they sparkled even when filled with water. Richards and Hartley Glass Company of Tarentum, Pa., made these wine, water, and cordial glasses around 1878 as part of a set of pressed glass in the Cupid and Venus pattern.*

would have been low and vulgar; to have drunk beer would have been to associate with immigrant working-class culture. On special occasions, such as a wedding, a birth, or a funeral, or on holidays such as Christmas, a ceremonial glass might be taken as a matter of ritual and tradition (fig. 14). Even these rites were declining, however, and in New York the old-fashioned New Year's eggnog of 1870 had all but disappeared by 1893. Middle-class men might stop off occasionally for a drink at a reputable drinking house or hotel, but middle-class women did not serve alcohol in the home. To have done so would have both violated standards of decency and raised questions about woman's role as the moral guardian of society. The middle classes were forced, in the name of propriety, either to give up alcohol or to drink sparingly—and guiltily.[15]

Even wine was condemned, although little was drunk; in 1885 annual consumption averaged only one-half gallon per person. Wine was imported, subject to tariff duties, and therefore expensive, and middle-class families had to be careful

[15] Hooker, *Food and Drink*, 272.

FIG. 15 *Wine merchants culti-vated respectability. An innocent child, a well-decorated dining room, and the pleasant conversation of a well-bred lady and gentleman are in harmony with the bottle of champagne featured prominently on this trade card for Great Western Champagne, New York, N.Y., 1886.*

about money. Wine appeared with regularity only at the tables of the wealthy, whose cellars were stocked with bottles purchased on European vacations. No doubt some middle-class Americans, especially nonevangelicals who continued to celebrate the eucharist with wine, imitated the upper classes by

W. J. Rorabaugh

FIG. 16 *The elegant way to serve ice water was from a pitcher that tilted. Decorations on this silver-plated pitcher, made by Reed and Barton in Taunton, Mass., in 1881, include snow flakes, icicles, and a floral motif.*

serving wine, but to do so went against their belief that it was important for the middle classes to set an example for people who were less well off (fig. 15). It would have been hypocritical for the middle classes to sip wine while telling the working classes to give up beer. Wrote one minister, "I propose to appeal to the magnanimity of the better classes in society to discontinue the moderate use of wines and liquors, for the benefit of those who are in danger of becoming confirmed inebriates." He hoped that such total abstinence would "render the custom of drinking unfashionable" and added, "it is a higher pleasure to know that by our self-denial we have saved others from sin and death than to enjoy the pleasures of which

Beer, Lemonade, and Propriety

FIG. 17 *Lemonade set, opal glass, United States, ca. 1870.*

we have denied ourselves." In the 1880s, this notion of sacrifice was sometimes compared to the sacrifices that had been made during the recent Civil War. For old-stock evangelical Protestants, calls to set a moral example were such an important part of religious tradition that they were difficult to resist. The result, then, was that propriety demanded abstinence from all alcoholic beverages.[16]

What middle-class Americans did drink at the dinner table was water, milk, or coffee. By the 1880s, these were the three most common beverages. Water had become a cult beverage among some antiliquor groups (fig. 16). It had been served ostentatiously at temperance-sponsored picnics and dinners, and temperance loyalists had paraded through the streets singing such lines as:

> Though Alcohol has had his day
> And great has been his slaughter,
> He's now retreating in dismay
> And victory crowns cold water.

Reformers had demanded pure public water supplies, and many American cities had built modern water systems that delivered sparkling, clear water direct to the tap in the house.

[16] Quotes are from J. P. Newman, "Self-Denial: A Duty and a Pleasure," in *Temperance Sermons Delivered in Response to an Invitation of the National Temperance Society and Publication House* (New York: National Temperance Society and Publication House, 1873), 102, 106, 110. This volume conveniently contains numerous other sermons that make the same point. On the wealthy, see Dannenbaum, *Drink and Disorder,* 216. On the Civil War, see William M. Taylor, "The Christian Serving His Generation," in *Temperance Sermons,* 392.

To drink milk it was necessary to own a cow—many small-town Americans did—or to have close access to one. Although coffee was imported, it was inexpensive and an increasingly important part of the American diet. The caffeine fitted in well with the emerging industrial age and the middle-class desire for an active participation in business that would bring financial success. Coffee was the new beverage of industry and propriety. Beer was not. On a warm summer's day, it was proper for the middle class to squeeze an imported lemon, stir in newly available pure white sugar, add a luxurious bit of ice, and serve lemonade (fig. 17).[17]

[17] Hooker, *Food and Drink*, 128–29, 272–73. The poem is in ibid., 129. But see Duis, *Saloon*, 95–96.

Technology and the Ideal

PRODUCTION QUALITY AND

KITCHEN REFORM IN

NINETEENTH-CENTURY AMERICA

DAVID W. MILLER

ETWEEN 1830 and 1920 a technological revolution occurred in the American kitchen which completely restructured its physical character and the type and number of utensils it contained. Within this period, women working in the home witnessed the introduction of new materials such as aluminum, new methods of storage such as refrigeration, new sources of power such as gas and electricity, and new forms of food preservation and distribution such as canning and the home delivery of milk in glass containers.

Recognizing the impact these technological changes could bring to daily life, a large number of women organized and published articles and books to try to guide women through them. As early as the 1840s, a group of women showed active

David W. Miller

FIG. 1 *"A Class in Cookery,*
Normal School of Household Arts,
Class of 1882," American Kitchen
Magazine: A Domestic Science
Monthly *(April–Sept. 1897).*

interest in improving the organization of the household; these
"domestic advisers" published their recommendations in hundreds of advice books, such as Catharine Beecher's 1841
Treatise on Domestic Economy, and were the progenitors of
domestic science (fig. 2). Arising in the late 1860s as a movement in land-grant colleges to offer formal instruction in home
economics, the study of domestic science was part of a rising
interest in science and nutrition. As one of the "helping professions" which women were encouraged to enter, home economics sought to apply science to the home but offered no
radical critique of women's roles therein.

ANOTHER GROUP of women organized and began to try to
influence the domestic sphere at roughly the same time. These
"material feminists," as historian Dolores Hayden has labeled
them, did call for an alternative social and political structure
for the home. Material feminists wanted to instigate "a grand

FIG. 2 *This illustration shows one end of a model kitchen proposed by Catharine Beecher and Harriet Beecher Stowe in their 1870 edition of* The American Woman's Home: or, Principles of Domestic Science. *Beecher, one of the early advocates of the application of "scientific" principles to the household, attributed the "disabilities and sufferings" of American women to the facts "that the honor and duties of the family state are not duly appreciated, that women are not trained for these duties as men are trained for their trades and professions, and that, as a consequence, family labor is poorly done, poorly paid, and regarded as menial and disgraceful." A systematized and functionally specific kitchen was viewed as essential to encourage and support the necessary training.*

domestic revolution" in which women would be paid for their household labor and in which the domestic environment and economy would be reorganized so that women could participate fully in the public life of the culture.[1] They envisioned a world in which applied natural and social science would improve the domestic lives of ordinary people, a world whose ideal state had been described by the American writer Edward Bellamy in his 1888 novel, *Looking Backward, 2000–1887*. In the novel, hero Julian West fell asleep in 1887 and woke up in Boston in the year 2000, full of questions about how society had changed:

"Who does your house-work, then?" I asked.

"There is none to do," said Mrs. Leete, to whom I had addressed this question. "Our washing is all done at

[1] The term "grand domestic revolution" appeared in Stephen Pearl Andrews, *The Baby World* (1855), reprinted in *Woodhull and Claflin's Weekly*, 8 June 1871, p. 10, and 28 October 1871, p. 12, and quoted in Dolores Hayden, *The Grand Domestic Revolution: A History of Feminist Designs for American Homes, Neighborhoods, and Cities* (Cambridge: M.I.T. Press, 1981), 2–3.

public laundries at excessively cheap rates, and our cooking at public shops. Electricity, of course, takes the place of all fires and lighting. We choose houses no larger than we need, and furnish them so as to involve the minimum of trouble to keep them in order. We have no use for domestic servants."

"What a paradise for womankind the world must be now!" I exclaimed.[2]

These women sought to improve the real situation of American women particularly in their kitchens, which one 1894 editorial in *New England Kitchen Magazine* called "the fortified intrenchments of ignorance, prejudice, irrational habits, rule of thumb, and mental vacuity."[3] By applying new scientific standards to the organization of housework—and, by extension, to the organization of the whole society—the material feminists proposed to liberate women in general, of all social classes, from tedious and time-consuming work. Saving labor among women would further the aims of democracy and would indeed produce social change of revolutionary proportions.

Yet the technological kitchen as it emerged in the nineteenth century was created within the context of opposition between the social goals of the material feminists and the inherent economic dynamics of profit-oriented mass production. Kitchen reform was not a planned, orderly process of positive changes upon which manufacturers and material feminists agreed, and in which material feminists exerted influence over production decisions. Ironically, kitchen utensil manufacturers and material feminists articulated the same rhetorical goal—freeing women from labor. Yet their notions about the source of this savings were dramatically different. Feminists believed that labor could only be saved if redundant household tasks were eliminated by collectivizing, on a local level, domestic chores such as laundering and cooking; as early as 1834 children's

[2] Edward Bellamy, *Looking Backward 2000–1887* (1888; reprint, Cambridge: Harvard University Press, 1967), 168–69.

[3] Professor Youmans, "Pen Pictures of All Sorts and Conditions of Kitchen," *New England Kitchen Magazine* 1 (April–Sept. 1894): 32.

STANYAN'S PATENT
BREAD MIXER & KNEADER.

Highly recommended wherever in use. No. 1, taking two to three quarts of flour, $3. No. 2, three to four quarts, $3.25. Forwarded upon receipt of price.
DUTCHER TEMPLE CO., Hopedale, Mass.
Money Order office, Milford, Mass.

FIG. 3 *Domestic advice periodicals frequently contained advertisements for new kitchen utensils. Stanyan's machine, advertised in the March 1881 issue of* The Household, *partly mechanized the laborious chores involved in making bread at home.*

author Caroline Howard Gilman had cited the need for municipally organized "grand cooking establishments" to save female household labor.[4] In the material feminists' vision, a group of women would work in well-organized kitchens with a minimum of well-designed utensils to prepare food that would be eaten in community dining clubs or delivered to private homes. Yet manufacturers, with the assistance of home economists such as Christine Frederick, located economy of labor in the "concentrated kitchen," one in every dwelling unit for every housewife or cook, who would work privately with the aid of hundreds of utensils (fig. 3).[5]

Two distinct aspects of emerging technology in the manufacture of consumer goods were the source of change in the nineteenth-century kitchen: applied science's successful control of metals, and, more important, the American acceptance of a new mode of fabrication—the mechanized, sequentially organized factory approach to production.

[4] Cited in Hayden, *Grand Domestic Revolution,* 248.
[5] *New England Kitchen Magazine* 2 (Oct. 1894–March 1895): 4.

David W. Miller

The seventeenth- and eighteenth-century kitchen had relied upon iron as the source of sturdy utensils for fireplace cooking. These utensils were often thick and heavy because they were cast using a crude system: a wooden form was wrapped with rope to construct a core creating the interior hollow of a pot, and layers of earth were then built up over the rope to form the pot wall. This earth was then covered with a layer of turf, the mud layer thereupon removed, and the hollow between the rope and the turf filled with molten iron. America's earliest extant example of such a pot, made in 1642 in Saugus, Massachusetts, was extremely heavy—twenty-four pounds—with walls more than one inch thick. Remaining fireplace utensils and flatware would have been made by the local blacksmith. Forged of iron, they tended to be heavy, as well as slow and uneven in their distribution of heat.

The end of the era of hand-cast or hand-forged utensils, and the first significant step toward fully mechanized production in the nineteenth century, was brought about by English and American toolmakers who invented rapidly moving machine parts. Henry Maudsley (1771–1831) divided the act of making objects into related sequential acts with his creation of Portsmouth block-making machinery for the Royal Navy in 1810. It was no longer necessary for skilled labor to produce and reproduce complex wooden blocks for raising the sails on ships.[6] The philosophical basis for the factory was thus laid. The city fathers of Birmingham, England—where, as early as 1769, Richard Lord had produced saucepans, warming pans, and kettles in a partially mechanized process that used water-powered, handmade drop hammers[7]—articulated this point of view in 1866:

> The old process of casting is utterly laid aside, and a more cheap and expeditious method is substituted. Artists of inventive minds and unwearied application have called in the aid of dies, presses, and one man can, in the same space of time, produce what on the old principle, would

[6] Eugene S. Ferguson, "Metallurgical and Machine-Tool Developments," in *Technology in Western Civilization,* ed. Melvin Kranzberg and Carroll W. Pursell, Jr. (New York: Oxford University Press, 1967), 1:275–78. A description of preindustrial casting processes can be found in John D. Tyler, "Cast-iron Cooking Vessels: Technological Features as a Guide to Date and Source," in *Antique Metalware,* ed. James R. Mitchell (New York: Universe Books, 1976), 220–24.

[7] W. C. Aitken, "Brass and Brass Manufacturers: The Early History of the Metal; The Introduction of the Manufacture of Brass into England; Its Development and Introduction into Birmingham; Progressive and Present Condition of the Manufacture," in *Birmingham Resources and Industrial History,* ed. Samuel Timmins (London, 1866), 292.

have required ten to perform, and by this improvement, beauty and elegance may be obtained without incurring the enormous expense which has hitherto accompanied them.[8]

A fellow Englishman and student of Maudsley named Joseph Whitworth (1803–87) understood the sequential ordering of machines in the Portsmouth system and developed uniform sets of accurate measures for all metal objects to perfect it.[9] This development meant that any machine could be linked in line using the same sizes of screw, the same thicknesses of metal, and so on; with it, Whitworth provided the technical ability to create the factory.

The contribution that made the factory a practical reality came from two Americans in Providence, Rhode Island. Based on Whitworth's approach, Joseph R. Brown and Lucien Sharpe created the first standard gauge for measuring metals, accurate to within one one-thousandth of an inch.[10] Most important and typical of the pragmatic American approach to technology, the gauges were inexpensive, as well as usable and accurate in a variety of situations. The Brown and Sharpe sliding caliper gauge went on sale in 1851 and revolutionized tooling work; any small metal-working shop could now provide accurate machinery which would be linked sequentially to make products rapidly and inexpensively.

This control of micromeasurement allowed the creation of machinery that could build all sizes of steam engines to replace water power, the only major power source previously used to make kitchen utensils for the American home.[11] Transition to the infant "American system" was rapid. Once fully powered and mechanized, utensil production rates literally rose several hundred percent in only five years; they then quadrupled and quadrupled again.[12]

The result was that, although the value of manufactured products was only $199 million in the United States in 1810, it exceeded $1,885 million by 1860.[13] This massive and success-

[8] Ibid., 293.

[9] Robert S. Woodbury, "Machines and Tools," in Kranzberg and Pursell, *Technology in Western Civilization*, 620–23.

[10] Ibid., 624–25.

[11] Timothy L. Dilliplane, "European Trade Kettles," in *Burr's Hill: A Seventeenth-Century Wampanoag Burial Ground in Warren, Rhode Island*, ed. Susan G. Gibson (Providence: Brown University Press, 1980), 2:79–83. Graphic illustration of this process can be found in Denis Diderot, *A Diderot Pictorial Encyclopedia of Trades and Industry*, ed. Charles Coulston Gillespie (New York: Dover Publications, 1959), vol. 1, plate 144.

[12] Courtney R. Hall, *History of American Industrial Science* (New York: Library Publishers, 1954), 1–54.

[13] Ibid., 21.

[14] Quantitative reports on American business growth during the adoption of mass production techniques are available from many sources. The most comprehensive are those contained in the United States Census and the related Government Departmental Yearly reports such as those produced by the Department of Agriculture. The Tenth Census, for example (Washington: Government Printing Office, 1883), ran to twenty-two volumes and included manufacturing schedules for firms with capital of $500 and greater. It gave vital information on the numbers and sex of workers, hours, wages, rhythms of annual operation, and value of product, thus allowing comparisons beyond the charting of production growth.

[15] T. K. Derry and Trevor I. Williams, *A Short History of Technology, from the Earliest Times to A.D. 1900* (New York: Oxford University Press, 1961), 598.

[16] Carroll W. Pursell, Jr., "Machines and Machine Tools, 1830–1880," in Kranzberg and Pursell, *Technology in Western Civilization*, 1:405.

[17] Jeannette Lasansky, *To Draw, Upset, & Weld: The Work of the Pennsylvania Rural Blacksmith, 1742–1935* (Lewisburg, Pa.: Union County Historical Society, 1980), 24–27.

[18] Edward Lucie-Smith, *The Story of Craft: The Craftsman's Role in Society* (Ithaca: Cornell University Press, 1981), 206.

ful restructuring of production technology caused output in many industries to mushroom.[14] In glass bottle manufacturing alone, it increased sixteen times.[15] In the well-documented shoe trade, the sewing machines perfected by Gordon McKay to join tops to soles increased output from 5 million pairs a year in 1864 to 25 million pairs by 1870; by 1895 production reached 120 million pairs annually. This new capability radically altered the availability of goods, dropping their cost enormously. For example, McKay's improvement decreased the cost of making shoes, previously done by hand, from seventy-five to only three cents per pair.[16]

Before 1830 most American towns had a blacksmith, who fabricated custom-made products on demand and whose list of customers typically ranged from 37 to 115 persons.[17] After 1830 the eager acceptance of the factory process destroyed these artisanal modes of producing ordinary kitchen equipment and changed consumer thinking at the same time. As Edward Lucie-Smith has observed,

> The handmade objects of pre-industrial society were in this sense unique—that each, however often the craftsman had performed a particular task, was a little different from the others. This quality of uniqueness was subconsciously present in people's minds. They bought for use, and they did not expect to use and discard. Now that expectation was in the process of being changed.[18]

This alteration in fabrication technology created an altered point of view: Americans exchanged the custom-made products of the skilled artisan for the uniform items created by mechanization. The changes in attitude that accompanied mechanization evolved into a highly enthusiastic, usually unquestioning, cultural orientation toward technology. Standardization, in becoming the norm, created new standards. The consumer's willingness to accept uniformity in goods almost implied a readiness to "use up" and discard these goods—as long as they could be easily and inexpensively replaced—because any one could be expected to perform as well as any other. Manufacturers understood this dynamic and hastened to realize it in producing goods for the kitchen.

But for American manufacturers to keep prices low, it was necessary to keep the expense involved in producing objects still lower. One no longer had only to satisfy one hundred customers; one had instead to allocate materials in large amounts to satisfy anonymous customers numbering in the hundreds of thousands. In this way, the change in production technology greatly altered not only the availability of goods, but also the very nature of the goods produced. This was the hidden structural and economic difficulty of volume production: to create many objects, tools to make them had to last a long time under much use and great duress. Also, the tools had to work accurately under the same conditions: when a part was struck, it had to release easily so that the next part of its type could be struck just as rapidly and as accurately. These tools, made of special steels and both difficult and expensive to make, limited the number of designs used for utensils. Most first used few designs, and the nature of these designs was controlled to create easy tooling and to avoid difficult release of formed pieces from the machine.

In this production necessity lay the irony of the American factory system. Although mechanization gave superior technical control of metals, the cost of tooling limited, both aesthetically and functionally, the utensils made. In providing Victorians with "the goods life," the tools used to create kitchen implements were made as inexpensively as possible; complex dies that would have provided high surface detailing, or dies made in multiple pieces that would have created subtle forms, were not used because of their expense.[19] As a result, utensils were often technically poor; although a wide variety of them was available, many simply did not function well.

No utensil exhibits the ultimate effects of this sensibility more clearly than the metal food mold.

The English-made copper food mold of five inches or more in

[19] Harold F. Williamson, "Mass Production for Mass Consumption," in Kranzberg and Pursell, *Technology in Western Civilization,* 1:678–92.

David W. Miller

FIG. 4 *This gelatin mold is a typi-cal example of the tin-lined copper tubed forms produced in England after the introduction of spinning as a major fabrication method in the early 1830s. Part of a 550-utensil set originally used by the first duke of Wellington at Apsley House in London, the mold features an en-graved ducal coronet, the initials "D.W.L." for "Duke of Welling-ton, London," and its shelf display number. Both hand and machine fabricated, the mold exhibits no manufacturer's or seller's marks. Courtesy Royal Pavilion, Brighton, England.*

[20] Henry James, *The Bostonians* (Hammondsworth, England: Penguin Books, 1978), 15.

[21] Mold manufacturers' catalogs reveal the pretensions surrounding the names of molds used for fancy presentations. A modern text which includes pages from such catalogs is Sally Kevill-Davies, *Jelly Moulds* (Guildford, Surrey, England: Lutterworth Press, 1983), 10–64.

[22] "Frozen Jewels," *American Kitchen Magazine: A Domestic Science Monthly* 7 (April–Sept. 1897): xiii.

height was a vital part of the Victorian kitchen on both sides of the Atlantic (fig. 4). For Victorians, the mold "spoke of habits and tastes," both literal and cultural.[20] It supplied decorative character to the table and implications about one's civilized habits and social position. Mold images of royalty, expensive pets, and famous lodgings such as the Belgrave, the Savoy, and the Carlton abounded.[21] In 1897, the vogue of the American social season was large molded gelatin or ice cream "gems," presented in such a way that guests would receive "a slice of flashing ruby, or . . . a spoonful of emeralds" (fig. 5).[22]

The development of the food mold was complemented by the availability of both machines and foods suitable for them. The modern crank ice cream machine, known as Johnson's Patent Ice Cream Freezer, was patented in 1848 by William G.

1. Turkey garnished with flowers
2. Sandwiches
3. Tongue
4. Open jelly with whipped cream
5. Jelly of two colors
6. Game pie. Aspic jelly in dish
7. Lobster
8. Ham

Centre stand for fruit and flowers. Custards in Tray

FIG. 5 *The frontispiece of the anonymous* Successful House-keeper *(Detroit, 1883) showed the foods recommended for a supper party. Sharing the position of importance with the "centre stand," or epergne, were two molded foods: at left, an "open jelly with whipped cream"; at right, a "jelly of two colors." Courtesy Jean Callan King.*

Young.[23] The Victorians had easy access to widely available commercial gelatins, such as Cox's of Edinburgh and Bird and Son's, which in 1837 also sold "Blanc Mange Powder, Custard and Pudding Powder." In America, the formula for Jello was patented in 1845 by Peter Cooper, who, along with Knox, Minute Brand, Plymouth Rock, and Bromangelon, also

[23] A. B. Marshall, *Ices Plain and Fancy: The Book of Ices*, introductions and annotations by Barbara Ketcham Wheaton (New York: Metropolitan Museum of Art, 1976), xviii.

David W. Miller

FIG. 6 *These molded courses were shown in Urbain Dubois's* Cuisine Artistique *(Paris, 1883). Courtesy David Miller.*

[24] I have often used gelatin manufacturers' promotional literature to ascertain the dates of company founding. See *Cox's Manual of Gelatine Cookery* (Edinburgh, 1938), 2, and *Pastry and Sweets for the Dinner and Supper Tables,* 21st ed. (Birmingham, England: Bird and Sons, Ltd., ca. 1904), 1. Information about Jello was obtained from the General Foods Consumer Center in White Plains, N.Y. The principal source of dating Knox, Minute Brand, Plymouth Rock, and Bromangelon was advertising in *The Ladies' Home Journal* between 1900 and 1920.

[25] English editions of haute cuisine publications available in America include Marie Antonin Careme, *The Royal Parisian Pastrycook and Confectioner,* ed. John Porter (London: F.J. Mason, 1834); Jules Gouffe, *The Book of Preserves* (London: Sampson, Low and Marston, 1871); and Jules Gouffe, *The Royal Book of Pastry and Confectionary* (London: Sampson, Low, Marston, Low and Searle, 1874).

sold regular gelatin.[24] Famous European chefs featured hundreds of molded presentations in English editions of texts available in America, such as Marie Antonin Careme's *Royal Parisian Pastrycook and Confectioner* (London, 1871), and *The Royal Book of Pastry and Confectionary* (London, 1874) (fig. 6).[25]

The ability to prepare molded foods was viewed as an important aspect of cooking skill among domestic scientists, although they were relatively less concerned about the imagery of molded foods than chefs were. By the turn of the century, many home economics courses included instruction in sweet and decorative courses such as "sugared entrements, [which] are considered almost as essential to a meal as the soup or the roast."[26] The 1897 course of study in domestic science in the Brookline, Massachusetts, public schools included "starch experiments, making of flour paste and of cornstarch molds, and use of commercial gelatins; Lemon jelly, snow pudding, Coffee jelly, coffee Bavarian cream."[27] Similarly, the Lynn, Massachusetts, school system offered classes in making cakes and molded pastry, while the less affluent Boston school system had students prepare molded small cakes "cast in iron gem pans."[28] In her 1896 Pratt Institute graduation thesis, "A Model School Kitchen," Miss Emily Merrill recommended the provision of nineteen molds—sixteen small and two large jelly molds and one large ice cream mold. Under Merrill's plan, sixteen students could only be taught this important skill effectively if each could practice with her own mold.[29]

Utensil manufacturers knew the importance of molded foods and responded by producing a wide array of forms. Mrs. A. B. Marshall, who sold molds in both the United States and England, offered more than 1,000 different designs (figs. 7 and 8).[30] Both general metal manufacturers and specialty mold makers for the ice cream and candy trade produced molds.

The food mold was not only a Victorian convention; it was also a Victorian invention. It could be fabricated easily only after the patenting of the process of stamping in 1769, which applied an engraved metal piece known as a die to form a piece of sheet metal.[31] The food mold was not produced by a specialist trade until 1824,[32] and throughout the nineteenth century, the finest molds available in America were made in England by such firms as Benham and Froud of London, or Ash Brothers

[26] C. Herman-Senn, *Luncheon and Dinner Sweets* (London: Ward, Lock and Co., Ltd., ca. 1910), 5.

[27] Alice P. Norton, "Course of Study in Domestic Science: Arranged for the Public Schools of Brookline, Mass.," *American Kitchen Magazine* 8 (Oct. 1897–March 1898): 25.

[28] Ibid., 23; Miss A. G. E. Hope, "Furnishings for Boston School Kitchens," *American Kitchen Magazine* 5 (April–Sept. 1896): 211–13.

[29] Emily Merrill, "A Model School Kitchen: Graduation Thesis, Pratt Institute," *American Kitchen Magazine* 6 (Oct. 1896–March 1897): 260–62.

[30] Marshall, *Ices Plain and Fancy*, viii.

[31] Aitken, "Brass and Brass Manufacturers," 292.

[32] *Critchett & Wood's London Directory*, 24th ed. (London, 1824), 51. Before 1824 no metal workers in either London or Birmingham were listed as specialists in cooking or confectionary molds. The first such listing appears in the above-mentioned source— "Brooke T., Fancy Mould Maker, 139 High Holborn." Two other such specialists were listed with Brooke in the 1826 *Pigot London Directory*—"Buhl, Jno. (and inventor for blancmange sellers and

60

David W. Miller

FIG. 7 *An Advertisement for*
Mrs. A. B. Marshall's Book of
Moulds *included specimens of*
English-made copper molds of
elaborate and intricate design. This
page from A. B. Marshall's Larger
Cookery Book of Extra Receipts
(London, 1902) shows only
thirteen of more than 1,000
marketed in both Europe and the
United States. Courtesy David
Miller.

pastry), 50 Old Compton St.,
Soho," and "Vanderlinden, Chas
(Jelly) 3 Devonshire St., Queen
Sq." London directory listings for
the specialist mold trade peaked in
1868; in that year, nine firms manufactured tin and copper molds. The
pewter mold trade kept separate
listings in London directories under
the heading "Ice Mould Makers."
These listings first appeared in
1856, when two firms appeared; six
firms were listed in the 1887 edition. Birmingham directories listed
craftsmen or firms only by the general job, such as "Japanner" or
"coppersmith." No headings for
mold makers existed.

and Heaton of Birmingham. These molds were technically
superior in a variety of ways (fig. 9). First, they were made of
copper, which excelled in its ability to transfer heat and cold
evenly. Second, the copper used was quite heavy, ranging from
sixteen to twenty gauge in thickness, or from .032 to .051

FIG. 8 *Mrs. Marshall's School of Cookery in London was advertised in the same volume in which a page of her molds appeared. The* London *newspaper* The Daily Chronicle *expressed the hopes of material feminists in its endorsement of the school: "Something like a revolution, or at all events a great change for the better, is being unostentatiously but gradually accomplished among cooks and in cooking, by the work carried on by Mrs. A. B. Marshall." Courtesy David Miller.*

inches. Third, they were usually spun. In 1838 the British Rev. Dionysus Lardner described spinning in his book *The Cabinet of Useful Arts:*

David W. Miller

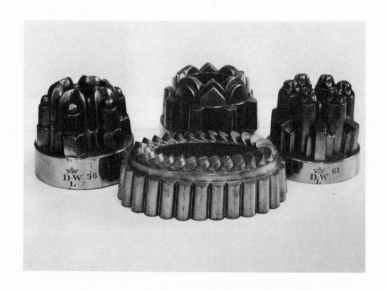

FIG. 9 *These four copper food molds from the duke of Wellington's collection are each marked with his initials, "L" (for London), a shelf display number, and the ducal crown. The molds in the rear are typical, being symmetrical and formed from one sheet of copper through machine spinning and stamping and final hand hammering. The center oval, number 29, is a later pieced mold comprised of top, side, and inner heat tube joined by soldering. All share the Victorian preference for geometric motifs and are lined with tin.*

upon a spindle rapidly revolving in a horizontal position is fixed a wooden chuck, or model of a pot or other article to be formed; or rather of so much of it as will allow the metal to slip off the wood after it has been closed upon it. A piece of sheet metal is cut with shears into a circular shape and of the size required; this is placed against the end of the revolving chuck and against the metal outside is applied a circular bit of wood having an indentation in the middle, where a center pin of obtuse form is screwed firmly upon it; thus placed and while it rapidly spins around, the workman applies various tools, either of hard wood or polished steel in the first place very gently, until by a succession of touches, he bends the plate over the model chuck.[33]

[33] Rev. Dionysus Lardner, *The Cabinet of Useful Arts: A Treatise on the Progressive Improvement and Present State of the Manufacture of Metals* (London: Longman, Arme, Brown, Green and Longmans, 1838), 3:105–6.

Spinning in this manner produced a smooth metal shell of even thickness, which was the outermost shape of the mold desired. The process was followed by stamping, which realized the details of the mold design. This contemporary description of the process is identical in principle to the more automated form of stamping in industry today, which uses power in place of gravity:

> The mechanical requisites are a stamp formed of a heavy mass of cast iron, which is sunk into the ground. From this, two cast iron uprights or pillars rise. On top of these is a transverse piece of metal, with an aperture in the centre, over which a pulley works. Over this pulley, with a groove in it, a rope works; to one end of the rope is attached a hammer or 'ram,' which slides between the pillars which act as guides; the other end of the rope is left free, and is used to raise the hammer. The die is attached to the bed of the stamp and held there by four screws; to the pulling hammer, a 'force' or convex copy of this die is attached. The piece of sheet metal to be stamped is laid on the die, the hammer is elevated by pulling the rope and it is then allowed to descend; the consequences of the blow is that the metal assumes the approximate form of the concavity sunk in the die.[34]

The combination of spinning and stamping actually strengthened the metal, giving the decorative forms rigidity and helping to avert denting and heat deformation. Most important, the longer method allowed for the creation of molds from a single sheet of metal, thus avoiding seams, which would collect food, which would weaken with use, and which were difficult to plate or coat with tin (the plating process was necessary to prevent the interaction of acids in foods with copper and steel).

In British mold manufacture, all machine processes were followed by hand planishing, which smoothed the outside surface of a metal piece by overlapping light blows from a springy hammer with a slightly convex face. Molds were then burnished, their surfaces pressed with great force with highly polished steel tools.[35] Burnishing completely smoothed the mold and gave sharp definition to decorative forms.

For asymmetrical or rectilinear molds, which could not be

[34] Aitken, "Brass and Brass Manufacturers," 304–9.
[35] Oppi Untracht, *Metal Techniques for Craftsmen* (Garden City, N.Y.: Doubleday, 1968), 249, 442.

FIG. 10 *This elaborate* garde-
manger *with its supply of food
molds appeared in Urbain Dubois,*
Cuisine Artistique *(Paris, 1883).
Courtesy David Miller.*

made of a single sheet of copper and thus could not be spun, all
seams in pieced construction were "keyed," or cut and joined
in a dovetail pattern and hammered for hardness. Keying produced a flat surface with very strong joints which provided
solders along a very large surface area. With no raised seams,
food could not collect and thereby potentially cause health
problems.

This combination of mechanized processes and hand work
allowed molds to reach heights of eight inches or higher, with
deep indentation on both the top and sides of two inches or
more. Motifs were visually impressive because they were
fully sculptural and often had finely delineated surface detail
(fig. 10). These English molds, well thought out and well executed, could realize to best advantage the dramatic effects inherent in the use of gelatin in cooking. Liner molds were
created which fitted inside larger molds, permitting a succession of layers of differently colored gelatins. The final molded
piece allowed one to view the layers through one another,
creating stunning effect. The 1925 edition of *Mrs. Beeton's
Cold Sweets* described the process:

By adding a little gold or silver leaf or a few drops of yellow, red or green vegetable coloring matter, considerable variety may be introduced at small costs. Pleasing effects may be produced by filling the projecting divisions of a mould with gold, silver or colored jelly, and the body of the mould with jelly that differs either in color or character. Of course, the colors must be blended artistically; bright colored creams like strawberry should be very simply decorated; and the creamy white of the almond or the delicate green of the pistachio nut embedded in the amber hued jelly with which the mould is lined, contrast favorably with chocolate, as also does finely flaked gold leaf.[36]

Both material feminists and the new ranks of college-educated domestic economists realized that the successful teaching of cooking skills required equipment that performed well. Unfortunately, this mandate forced the exclusion of many poorly tooled American molds. Because American manufacturers used different mechanized fabrication methods than their British counterparts, the initial costs of molds were lowered, but the nature of the finished product was also changed entirely.

In their choice of materials for metal molds, American manufacturers made their selections based entirely on ease of fabrication (fig. 11a and b). The uniform result was the selection of soft sheet steel (fifteen to thirty percent carbon) for molds. Steel's high tensile strength—the ability to resist elongation without breaking—made it possible to shape it with a single blow. It therefore required less labor to form than copper did, and molds made from it could be produced faster than copper ones, which required slower successive stamps. Products made of steel, whether tinned or enameled, were poor heat conductors and prone to rust.[37] Nonetheless, they dominated the market through large-scale production by general

[36] Isabella Mary Beeton, *Mrs. Beeton's Cold Sweets* (London: Ward, Lock and Co., Ltd., 1925), 10.

[37] Earl Lifshey, *The Housewares Story* (Chicago: National Housewares Manufacturers Association, 1973), 150–58.

David W. Miller

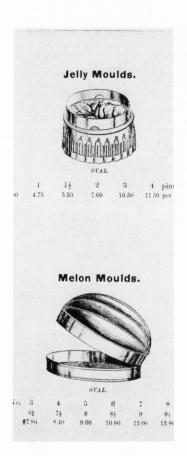

Jelly Moulds.

OVAL.

| 1 | 1½ | 2 | 3 | 4 | pint |
|)0 | 4.75 | 5.50 | 7.00 | 10.50 | 11.50 | per |

Melon Moulds.

OVAL.

No. 3	4	5	6	7	8
6¼	7½	8	8¼	9	9¼
$7.80	8.40	9.60	10.80	12.00	13.80

Rice Moulds.

FLUTED.

No.	1	2	3	pints
	3	4	6	per doz.
	$9.00	10.50	12.00	

Ice Cream Moulds.

FLUTED.

| 4 | 5 | 6 | pints. |
| $13.20 | 13.80 | 15.00 | per doz. |

FIG. 11a and b *Only four food molds appeared in the 1874* Illustrated Catalogue of Goods *produced by Sidney Shepard and Company of Buffalo, N.Y., proprietor of the Buffalo Stamping Works. All were low in height and relatively simple in design; the raised botanical decoration on the jelly mold appears on the top surface and was probably machine stamped.*

38 *Dover Stamping Co.: Manufacturers and Dealers in Tinner's Hardware & Furnishing Goods* (1869; reprint, Princeton, N.J.: Pyne Press, 1971), x–xvii.

metal companies such as the Dover Stamping Company of Boston, for it was considered culturally necessary to have equipment to make molded foods.[38] For the middle-class home, stamped steel was the material of choice because, being easily fabricated in volume, it was readily available at affordable prices.

To achieve tall, vertical molds, English manufacturers had used thick gauges of copper to compensate for the metal's thinning during spinning and stamping. American manufacturers instead used rapid forming steel, which produced lower forms in which the base diameter and height of the mold were nearly

FIG. 12 *Pudding or ice cream molds, United States, steel and enameled steel, ca. 1900.*

equal. These dimensions allowed uniform pressure on the stamped surface, and designs for molds were chosen so that they too would distribute pressure evenly. For the most part, then, designs were simple and symmetrical because, as one twentieth-century technical bulletin has put it, "flanges and other projections are costly to attain. Uneven shapes, severe bends often result in production difficulties. Relatively sharp corners are to be avoided."[39] In production, oval and round forms dominated, with decoration generally placed upon the top plane because stamps strike from above. Motifs were low, with rounded edges and soft detailing to permit both easy tooling and easy release from the machine. American manufacturers used only machine processes; all intermediate steps, such as spinning and hand forming, were eliminated. Liner molds were not even fabricated, for they would have cost as much to produce as the primary mold (fig. 12).

Through their selection of fabrication process, American manufacturers inadvertently removed important sculptural characteristics from the molds and negated the most important

[39] S. E. Rusinoff, *Manufacturing Processes, Materials and Production* (Chicago: American Technical Society, 1962), 26.

FIG. 13 *This chromolithograph of a dessert table, featuring several molded foods, appeared in Elizabeth F. Ellet's* New Cyclopaedia of Domestic Economy *(Norwich, Conn., 1873).*

social role they were designed to perform—to provide a dramatic touch, "to decorate the table and stimulate conversation." It was probably through unsuccessful trials that women became aware that American-made food molds could not create the proper effects on the table and thereby reflect the skill and good taste of the hostess. As historian Louise Belden has noted, "The more originality a hostess displayed in her molded dishes, the greater the number of favorable comments made by her guests. If inventive in varying the details, [she] could score high" (fig. 13).[40]

Combined with this inability to create molded foods of interesting shapes, steel molds created problems in cooking—hot spots, surface burning, and possible contamination from rust or chipped enamel—that increasingly affected both private homemakers and domestics. Successful molded dishes were much more difficult to achieve with steel molds than they were with copper ones. These deficiencies contributed to the decline

[40] Louise C. Belden, *The Festive Tradition: Table Decoration and Desserts in America, 1650–1900* (New York: W. W. Norton and Co., 1983), 157, 158.

in use of molds so that by the middle of the twentieth century all but one American Victorian mold company had gone out of business, and general metal manufacturers' mold catalogs included no more than five designs.[41] Ultimately, food molds ceased to be a major source of industrial utensil income.

This feature of the American factory system created a specific point of conflict between manufacturers and material feminists. Food molds were not the only kitchen utensil that failed to perform efficiently and to save women's labor. A great many devices were so inefficient that they actually created more work for the housewife. The perfect example is the Zeppelin potato baker made by the TMW Company, which was an egg-shaped metal device that opened to reveal a spike on which to impale a single potato for even baking. Yet when nearly half of all late nineteenth-century American households had five or more occupants, a hostess would certainly have needed to purchase numerous Zeppelin bakers. It is not clear, in any event, that baking potatoes evenly was perceived as a potential problem by nineteenth-century American cooks.[42]

Material feminists wanted manufacturers to produce utensils that could be used in collective cooking, thereby reducing the number of utensils needed for housekeeping by individual women. According to Hayden, they succeeded in influencing the creation of at least twenty services that delivered cooperatively prepared hot food to private homes, and of at least thirteen community dining clubs between 1869 and 1921.[43] In terms of quality, the specialized cooking apparatus that feminists envisioned for group use would have needed to be of great size, made of heavy metals, feature specific construction details to make them easier to use, and require the manufacture of objects such as stands, transport platforms, and large heat sources. In effect, material feminists hoped to keep alive the possibilities of custom-designed utensil manufacture so that kitchen reform, in part realized through innovative equipment design, could occur.

Yet manufacturers could profit only when they produced in

[41] David W. Miller, "Commercial Aspects of Current Food Mold Production" (Paper for Revere Copper and Brass Historic Mold Project, 1980). As of 1980, eighteen firms were found to be deriving income from metal food mold production. Nine were American, and nine were based in other countries. Generally, their designs fell within a very narrow range of traditional food presentations, especially the Kugelhopf-savarin, charlotte, or square and tower ice cream bombes. The average line included six molds; only one company provided molds in as many as eighteen different designs.

[42] Linda C. Franklin, "Letters," *Kitchen Collectibles News* 1, no. 3 (May–June 1984): 45.

[43] Hayden, *Grand Domestic Revolution*, 345–55.

large volume, and for them the most advantageous marketing situation was at least one fully equipped kitchen per dwelling unit. Indeed, the more kitchen implements a woman bought, the larger the manufacturers' profit. The direct mercantile response to calls for kitchen reform was to create innumerable utensil novelties, all in the ostensible interest of saving labor for women. For manufacturers, the entire concept of the kitchen became one of a "utensilized" entity.

Powered machines produced an enormous number of kitchen utensils which essentially, like the machines themselves, separated food preparation into self-contained mechanical processes. In doing this, the physical structure of the kitchen was changed. Instead of a wall dominated by a fireplace, by 1830 the iron range was a movable, factory-made object that could be placed anywhere. Similarly, the cold or root cellar, a necessity for general food preservation, was replaced by the ice box after 1827. Individual dairy rooms and smokehouses were no longer necessary when factory-processed products became available in mass-produced containers of tin or glass. The larder as a meat and fresh-food storage room ceased to be an architectural necessity by 1920.

The manufacturing process made it possible to convert any room with access to piped water and power—first, after 1860, in the form of gas, and then (by 1882 in New York City) in the form of electricity—into a kitchen. Electricity in fact was promoted with the same promise that utensils were—it offered freedom from labor—and it was a promise whose charm struck a good number of home economists. An 1896 issue of *The American Kitchen Magazine: A Domestic Science Monthly* proclaimed that with the aid of electric appliances, a woman would find cooking "her pleasure to attend to; and then we shall be vexed no longer with proffered solutions of the domestic problem, for there will be no domestic problem to solve."[44]

Numerous kitchen utensils were patented and produced,

[44] Estelle M. H. Merrill, "Electricity in the Kitchen," *American Kitchen Magazine* 5 (April–Sept. 1896): 60.

and they were advertised with identical rhetoric. By 1842 more than 200 patents had been granted for washing machines alone.[45] One of these, the "Sabin," was advertised in an 1849 issue of *American Agriculturist* to be capable of cleaning clothes and fine linens in only three minutes. When hand washing typically took an entire day, the fact that the Sabin was claimed to do "the ordinary washing of a private family . . . in about an hour" was strongly appealing.[46]

Even though many of the kitchen devices offered for sale were technically quite weak in actual performance, they were patented and fabricated in great quantities. Even instruments for simple tasks were produced in incredible variety for sale in the marketplace. A prime example is the beater for mixing. In 1870, and again in 1873, Nathaniel C. Miller of Strausberg, Pennsylvania, received patents for "egg beaters"; he described the 1873 improved version to be "a wire blade or paddle for better breaking or dividing the egg or other things to be beaten. . . . The hand wheel being turned, imparts motion to the pinion, imparting a vibrating motion to the same, which enables a person to perfectly beat an egg in thirty-five seconds."[47]

Miller's egg beater was in competition with the Earles Patent Egg Beater, claimed by the 1869 Dover Stamping Company catalog to be "the simplest, . . . the most effective Egg beater made. Held in the hand with an immovable rest, it stands firmly wherever placed, and will beat eggs with greater rapidity than any other." Another competitor for both was Munroe's Patent Egg Beater, which Dover Stamping observed "is too well known to the public to need our commendation." Finally, there was the Dover Patented Egg Beater, claimed to be the only egg beater with a "third pinion" and "the Mother of Them All—Guaranteed to outwear any other egg beater made" (fig. 14).[48]

Often, the technical reason offered for the superiority of an implement made little if any sense. The makers of Hersey's Patent Double Action Apple Parer, winner of the first premium

[45] Pursell, "Machines and Machine Tools," 406.
[46] *American Agriculturist* 8 (Nov. 1849): xi.
[47] Linda C. Franklin, "Patent Record," *Kitchen Collectibles News* 1, no. 1 (Jan.–Feb. 1984): 6.
[48] *Dover Stamping Co.: Manufacturers and Dealers,* 140, ix.

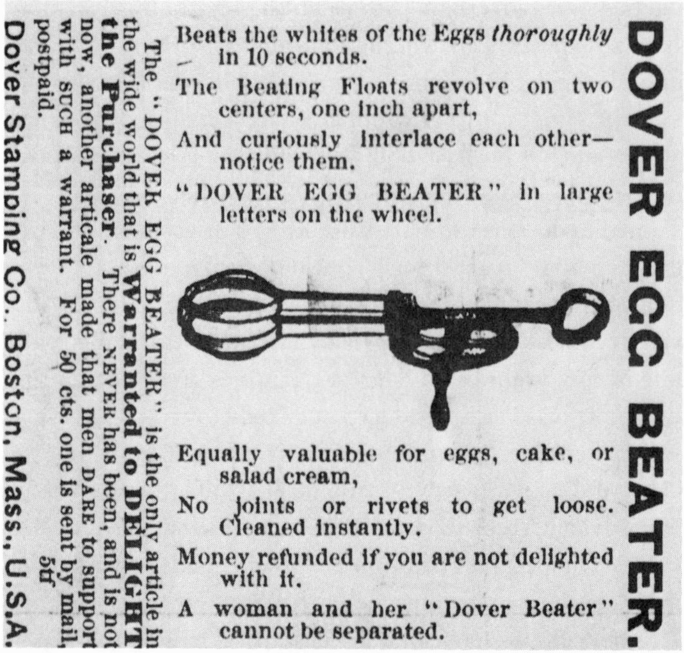

FIG. 14 *This advertisement for the Dover egg beater, manufactured by Dover Stamping Company of Boston, appeared regularly in issues of* The Household, *a monthly "domestic journal . . . devoted to the interests of the American housewife," throughout the late 1870s and early 1880s.*

Beats the whites of the Eggs *thoroughly* in 10 seconds.

The Beating Floats revolve on two centers, one inch apart,

And curiously interlace each other— notice them.

"DOVER EGG BEATER" in large letters on the wheel.

Equally valuable for eggs, cake, or salad cream,

No joints or rivets to get loose. Cleaned instantly.

Money refunded if you are not delighted with it.

A woman and her "Dover Beater" cannot be separated.

The "DOVER EGG BEATER" is the only article in the wide world that is **Warranted to DELIGHT the Purchaser.** There NEVER has been, and is not now, another article made that men DARE to support with SUCH a warrant. For 50 cts. one is sent by mail, postpaid.

Dover Stamping Co., Boston, Mass., U.S.A.

DOVER EGG BEATER.

by the New England Agricultural Society in 1864, claimed that it was "the only Machine ever Patented which pares an Apple with the reverse movement of the Knife!"[49]

Like molds, many utensils were created for the elaborate presentation of foods, such as cake and sandwich cutters in fanciful designs, or long-handled molds for shaping mashed potatoes on the plate. These at least served a particular cultural interest, yet many devices were manufactured which were totally unnecessary for cooking (fig. 15). Some domestic advisers clearly felt large numbers of implements to be necessary. In 1881 Maria Parloa recommended a minimum of 139 utensils in her list of necessary kitchen tools in *Miss Parloa's New Cook Book,* where she stated that "the housekeeper will find that there is continually something new to be bought."[50] Mary J. Lincoln, first principal of the Boston Cooking School, presented a list of 373 pieces for the well-equipped kitchen in

[49] Ibid., 112.
[50] Maria Parloa, *Miss Parloa's New Cook Book: A Guide to Marketing and Cooking* (Boston: Estes and Lauriat, 1881), 66.

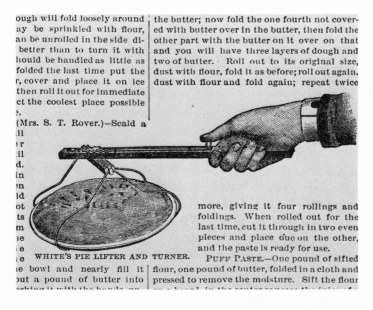

FIG. 15 *In her "Practical House-keeping" column in* The Ladies' Home Companion *(15 April 1888), domestic adviser Eliza R. Parker endorsed White's pie lifter and turner as she suggested how to make good pastry and pies. "For handling pies in the oven," she wrote, "White's pie lifter will be found a great convenience, as pies can be readily moved with it without spilling the juice or burning the hands. Cooks using it cannot fail to be pleased with it." Later lists of kitchen equipment appearing in domestic science cookbooks fail to recommend a pie lifter, however.*

the April 1894 issue of *New England Kitchen Magazine*.[51] Utensil stores such as F. A. Walker of Boston offered illustrated catalogs showing more than 1,000 plates of "useful and ornamental goods for the parlor, dining room, kitchen and laundry." Walker actually offered double the number of items illustrated in its catalog; the company's house furnishings guide of 1871 recommended the purchase of 429 utensils.[52]

Throughout the nineteenth century, American manufacturers strove to keep costs low on machine tooling; engineers designed forms that were inexpensive to produce, not that realized the best possible utensil. The result, in production terms, was that machine prerogatives went unmodified. Rivets and other joining systems, for example, were not placed for maximum strength but to produce the fewest number of procedures in the factory. Whereas two rivets would hold a spatula blade in place so that the implement would still function if one rivet sheared off or loosened, one central rivet created a spatula that was fifty percent cheaper to produce. When the single rivet on such a spatula loosened, the blade

51 Mary J. Lincoln, "Kitchen Furnishings," *New England Kitchen Magazine* 1 (April–Sept. 1894): 157–61.
52 *F. A. Walker & Co., Illustrated Catalogue of Useful and Ornamental Goods Suitable for the Parlor, Dining-Room, Kitchen, and Laundry* (Boston, 1871), 127–29.

would pivot sideways, making the utensil entirely unusable. Such manufacturing practices produced not one sale but a second replacement sale, which discouraged improvements in production.

The difference in approaches to factory manufacture led to the creation of two classes of kitchen goods—American-made, for the consumer on a limited budget, and imported. Because workers' organizations in European countries influenced governments to control mechanization and thereby protect the jobs of laborers, the factory system was slower to take complete hold of production. Skilled workers were abundant, and they managed to produce products of high quality in large numbers. In F. A. Walker's catalogs, attention to production detail was synonymous with "imported" across the board. The section on "Plain Tinware" in its 1871 catalog began with a precautionary paragraph:

> Many of these goods are imported by us, and are of much stronger material and finer finish than the American. The American goods are struck by a single blow, and the texture of the goods is thus injured; while the imported goods are spun up and annealed and will outwear the American.[53]

F. A. Walker's japanned ware, which included storage tins, canisters, and tubs, was presented with the same apologia: "This department is very extensive, and to obtain first-class goods, we are obliged to import them." Even basic items included in the "Hardware and Table Cutlery" were so distinguished. "We import the finest goods made in this line direct from the best English and French manufactories," the 1871 catalog stated.[54]

Material feminists failed to recognize that the manufacturing system that had taken hold in the United States was incapable of producing the utensils they wanted and thus could not equip kitchens that would actually save labor for the majority of women. Creating utensils for cooperative kitchens

[53] Ibid., 19.
[54] Ibid., 31, 55.

would obviously not produce increasing income for manufacturers, particularly when the design solutions for such utensils could require unique production capabilities. According to Hayden, the apparent confusion among material feminists about technical changes in the American factory system actually left them "vulnerable to fierce attacks from large industrial corporations who had an immediate economic interest in preventing women from socializing domestic work."[55]

The impetus for utensil-related kitchen reform lay in two fields that were born during the late Victorian period—home economics (or domestic science) and social work. In keeping with new developments in nutritional science and sanitation, professionals in both fields sought to reorganize both diet and the physical environment of the kitchen. Material feminists sought a further end—the creation of a classless society where kitchen tasks were naturally shared across all previous social boundaries. In an article entitled "Cooperative Housekeeping" in a 1903 issue of *House Beautiful*, home economist Mary Hinman Abel described how her generation of reformers envisioned the public housing of the future after Edward Bellamy had presented his own view in *Looking Backward*:

> A chef . . . master of his art, and also of the new knowledge in nutrition now available; one kitchen fire instead of fifty; . . . the peripatetic housemaid and all other workers responsible to a bureau; the house heated from a central station, where a competent engineer shall extract from each pound of coal all the heat it should yield.[56]

The home economics movement maintained that applying scientific standards to the kitchen necessitated two kinds of action. The first was to create cooking schools "to give instruction in scientific cookery, and to disseminate information of hygienic methods in the culinary art to all classes of society." The first such school was the Boston Cooking School, created by the Women's Education Association of Boston in 1879. In 1893, 889 persons received instruction in "cookery, chem-

[55] Hayden, *Grand Domestic Revolution*, 8.
[56] Cited in ibid., 135.

David W. Miller

FIG. 16 *"Kitchen Laboratory, Boston Normal School of House-hold Arts," photograph in* New England Kitchen Magazine: A Domestic Science Monthly *1 (April–Sept. 1894).*

[57] "The Boston Cooking School," *New England Kitchen Magazine* 1 (April–Sept. 1894): 3, 7.

[58] "Notes from the Field," *American Kitchen Magazine* 3–7 (April 1895–March 1898). This column, which presented correspondence from teachers trained in cookery and domestic science, provides some indication of the number and founding dates of programs established across the United States up to the turn of the century.

[59] Harvey Levenstein, "The New England Kitchen and the Origins of Modern American Eating Habits," *American Quarterly* 32, no. 4 (Fall 1980): 374.

istry, marketing pedagogy and the physiology of digestion."[57] Cooking schools were established in most major eastern cities, as well as in a number of schools and colleges across the country (fig. 16). The Boston, Brookline, and Lynn public schools in Massachusetts, the Armour Institute in Chicago, and Miss Master's School in Dobbs Ferry, New York, included a cooking-oriented domestic science program in their curricula. Many western and midwestern agricultural and land grant colleges also offered instruction in scientific cookery.[58]

The second way to effect kitchen reform was the public kitchen, to be established across the country on the model of the Rumford Kitchen that had been featured in the Massachusetts pavilion at the World's Columbian Exposition in Chicago in 1893. The Rumford Kitchen had been established by the home economist Mary Hinman Abel and Ellen Swallow Richards, a sanitary chemist who had been the first female graduate of the Massachusetts Institute of Technology and who, in 1884, became the first woman to be appointed to the MIT faculty.[59] The Rumford Kitchen, Richards wrote, included "all the equipment of a scientific laboratory designed to extract the maximum amount of nutrition from food sub-stances and the maximum heat from fuel."[60]

Richards's experience had come directly from a public kitchen which she and Abel had established in Boston in 1890—the New England Kitchen, at 142 Pleasant Street. Its goal was also "to provide superior nutrition for the poor through preparing food by better methods than those commonly in use," a goal shared by similar kitchens established in New York and at Jane Addams's Hull House in Chicago shortly afterward. To achieve this end, Richards experimented with a wide variety of utensils, including "many of the most scientific cooking appliances of the nineteenth century."[61] One of these was the Aladdin oven, a rectangular wooden box oven insulated with asbestos which relied on kerosene lamps to supply the heat for even, slow cooking. Invented in the late 1880s by Boston businessman Edward Atkinson, the Aladdin oven saved considerable fuel but never reached high temperatures. The food most appropriate for preparation in it was soup or stew, which Atkinson thought to be the best foods for the working class because they were protein- and fat-rich as well as economical. Soups and stews would therefore not only improve the health of immigrant workers, but would also allow them to save money on food.[62]

The experimental public kitchens were directly patterned on MIT labs and even used the same glassware and gas jet designs. Similarly, the space was spare, easy to clean, and functional; essentially, this kitchen was the forerunner of the hotel kitchen.[63] Specialized manufacturers did produce equipment for public kitchens, geared to prepare food daily for 500 or more people—people who the material feminists expected would pay for their scientifically prepared fare, just as they paid for commonly prepared food at public eating houses.

More widespread use of specially prepared cooking equipment in public kitchens never occurred, however, chiefly for two reasons. One was dietary: immigrant populations ap-

[60] Richards, cited in Hayden, *Grand Domestic Revolution,* 151.

[61] Ellen Swallow Richards, "Count Rumford and the New England Kitchen," *New England Kitchen Magazine* 1, no. 1 (April 1894): 7, 11.

[62] Edward Atkinson, "The Art of Cooking," *Popular Science Monthly* 36 (Nov. 1889): 18–19; Levenstein, "The New England Kitchen," 371–72.

[63] Captain M. P. Wolff in the British publication *Food for the Million: A Plan for Starting Public Kitchens* (London: Sampson, Low, Marston, Searle and Rivington, 1884) proposed using all the specialized equipment of the hotel trade in the public kitchen. Cited in Hayden, *Grand Domestic Revolution,* 162.

parently did not like the taste of the scientifically prepared foods. Moreover, at least at the New England Kitchen, the menus routinely featured beef broth, "Pilgrim succotash," creamed codfish, various chowders, baked beans, Indian pudding, and corn and oatmeal mush—"hardly a bill of fare to attract Boston's Irish and French Canadians," as Harvey Levenstein has noted, "not to mention Italians, Jews, and Central and Eastern Europeans."[64]

The other reason why cooperative kitchens failed is that their organizers were unable to muster the public and financial support needed to underwrite their experimental utensils, and therefore could not continue to operate the kitchens. As Ellen Richards said in 1894, "For a charity that feeds the hungry there is no lack of the bounty of good people; but it is safe to say that not many could be found who would be willing to give liberally and unrestrictedly to carry on a scientific experiment in the hope of learning how the people might be better fed."[65] Manufacturers, for their part, clearly saw no continuing market in the material feminists' fantasies and they concentrated instead on areas of assured economic return.

Thus, the specialized utensils needed in public kitchens or on wagons designed to deliver cooked food were neither widely produced nor technically perfected. They remained the substance only of feminist novels. In *What Diantha Did,* a serial novel written in 1909 and 1910 by Charlotte Perkins Gilman, the heroine described the technical wonders of equipment provided by wealthy philanthropic Viva Weatherstone for Diantha Bell's cooked food service. In the novel, Miss Weatherstone displayed a new food container she had ordered in Paris.

> They lifted it in amazement—it was so light.
>
> "Aluminum" she said, proudly. "Silver plated—new process! And bamboo at the corners you see. All lined and interlined with asbestos, rubber fittings for silverware, plate racks, food compartments—see?"

[64] Hayden, *Grand Domestic Revolution,* 159; Levenstein, "The New England Kitchen," 385.

[65] Richards, "Count Rumford," 8.

She pulled out drawers, opened little doors, and rapidly laid out a table service for five. . . .

"What lovely dishes," said Diantha.

"You can't break them, I tell you," said the cheerful visitor, "and dents can be smoothed out in any tin shop. . . ."[66]

On a more practical level, material feminists did speak out in the press on the worth of various kitchen utensils in private homes. In an 1895 edition of *American Kitchen Magazine,* a kitchen garbage drier which had been invented by a Dr. Durgin, chairman of the Boston City Board of Health, was evaluated and described this way:

It consists of a perforated sheet iron basket, with a tight bottom and a capacity of 3 or 4 quarts. It is inserted into an expanded section of the stove pipe and allows the hot air and smoke to pass on all sides of the basket. It is easily withdrawn from its position and replaced with one hand. It will receive the garbage as it occurs several times a day, and needs to be emptied but once in 24 hours. The garbage dries to a charcoal without burning, and it becomes an excellent fuel for kindling the fire in the morning. It does not compromise the use of the stove, interfere with the draft, require more fuel or cause any odors.[67]

The garbage drier was proposed to affect the public good because, in addition to its stated sanitary advantages, it would reduce the costs of garbage collection—which, in Boston, amounted to more than $182,000 in 1894. More important, the device allowed material feminists to make a connection between its invention and the fulfillment of women's goals:

The question of garbage disposal has grown to be one of the most vital with which large cities have to deal. . . . It now appears as if the opportunity to solve this question would be put into the hands of women. . . . Already, the

[66] Gilman, quoted in Hayden, *Grand Domestic Revolution,* 220–21.

[67] *American Kitchen Magazine* 3 (April–Sept. 1895): 102–3.

mayor of Chicago has appointed a woman as inspector in one ward of that city. Miss Addams, through her work at Hull House is especially fitted to attack this problem, and lead the way for other women to follow. . . . The house-cleaning proclivities of women have long been the jest of the newspapers, and the only wonder is that they have not been given this opportunity before to show their ability on a slightly larger scale. What a pity that so much force has been wasted in overdoing this work in our houses, when our larger home, the town or city, has had need of just this energy.[68]

Although manufacturers did not spend time and money to develop the types of utensils that material feminists envisioned, they did recognize the advantage of aligning themselves with the more moderate goals articulated by domestic scientists. They borrowed the teaching format developed for cooking schools and home economics curricula and applied them to the promotion of kitchen goods.

The 1894 World's Food Fair in Boston, for example, filled six acres with equipment displays and included presentations by such firms as Chase and Sanborn, S. S. Pierce Company, Joseph Burnett and Company, and Swift and Company. Sponsored by the Boston Retail Grocers' Association, the food fair's proclaimed goal was to "teach the public to know and demand the best" (fig. 17). Its real goal, however, was to create brand identification among consumers, and it did this by using the graduates of domestic science's cooking schools to run the booths and lend an aura of expertise. As *New England Kitchen Magazine* noted, "The brigade of cooks and attendants in dainty gowns, white aprons and caps, doing their work of mixing, cooking and serving, without making a 'mess' of themselves or their surroundings, teach a lesson that many surely note and follow." Indeed, the headquarters of *New England Kitchen Magazine* was in the booth of the Hygienic Refrigerator Company and the company that produced the Harkinson

[68] Ibid., 102.

FIG. 17 *"Home Department of the World's Food Fair," photograph in* New England Kitchen Magazine 2 *(Oct. 1894–March 1895).*

kitchen cabinet table, both of whose products the magazine recommended as superior. "The experienced housekeepers invariably stopped on their way to examine this table," the editors noted. "They can see at a glance what a marvelous saving of time, effort and strength can be affected by using this concentrated kitchen, where every utensil and all materials are at hand."[69]

Such overt interaction between mercantilists and feminist ideologues provoked *New England Kitchen Magazine* to state hopefully, "The influence of the cooking schools is apparent in all the exhibits, and the presence of their graduates in the booths of the manufacturers may be but the beginning of a new departure in the grocery business. . . ." Yet even *New England Kitchen Magazine* was aware of the potential abuse of this alliance:

[Such exhibits have] been seized upon in some instances, by the business adventurer, who runs it merely as a "show" out of which to extract as much money as possible, and this fact has brought discredit upon the name, and has aroused a prejudice against such affairs in the

[69] *New England Kitchen Magazine* 2 (Oct. 1894–March 1895): 4, 7, 7–8.

minds of many. But, . . . the honest and intelligent manufacturers and dealers have become interested, and . . . others who belong to neither class, but who might be styled social missionaries, have come to realize the great possibilities of these expositions.[70]

Domestic scientists increasingly used grocers' associations and utensil manufacturers both as sources of capital and as a commercial platform. Manufacturers, in their turn, used the scientifically oriented vocabulary of domestic science to increase sales. This 1894 advertisement for the "Anti-Burning or Iron Clad Salamander Bottom for Sheet Metal Kitchen Utensils" is a case in point. This metal ring, which raised a pot above a direct flame to prevent its contents from burning, was described this way:

This auxiliary or independent bottom is a dish shaped structure, centrally concavo-convex in form, with a series of corrugations or grooves extending radially from a central boss to the outer lower edge of the rim or flange, which receives the vessel to which the auxiliary or independent bottom is applied. Openings are provided at suitable intervals in the base of this auxiliary or independent bottom for the purpose of admitting air. Demand for these articles is almost unprecedented in the history of kitchen utensils.[71]

Such hyperbole confuses the practical definition of the product, yet it seemed necessary in order to conform with the language material feminists used as they tried to apply the objectivity of science to the jobs women had to do. Many advertisements in domestic science magazines relied on similarly pseudoscientific language. Yet among manufacturers, it was an empty language: their economic imperative overruled any serious consideration of social ideology. Using the skills of home economists such as Christine Frederick, consumption

[70] Ibid., 3.
[71] Ibid. 1 (April–Sept. 1894): 120–21.

was stressed over the real technical virtues of any utensil. In her 1929 book *Selling Mrs. Consumer,* dedicated to Herbert Hoover and addressed to advertising executives, Frederick emphasized the value of marketing to women's suggestibility, "passivity and inferiority complexes."[72]

Frederick's espoused goals did not effectively differ from those of utensil manufacturers, who sought to realize the greatest possible profit by equipping private homes with as many utensils as possible. After all, as Frederick observed, "there is a direct and vital business interest in the subject of young love and marriage. Every business day approximately 5000 new homes are begun; new 'nests' are constructed and new family purchasing units begin operation. . . . the founding and furnishing of new homes is a major industrial circumstance in the United States."[73]

What had been a loose association between manufacturers and the advocates of domestic science in the 1880s had become paid advocacy by the 1920s. What began as urgings from material feminists for manufacturers to develop efficient, durable, high-quality utensils for cooperative kitchens had been recast into Frederick's "consumptionism," what she called "the greatest idea that America has to give to the world."[74]

Frederick's "consumptionism" was the graphic repudiation of the material feminists' belief that by restructuring spaces such as the kitchen and by redesigning the utensils within it women might be freed of their kitchen tasks and thereby permitted to become more effective participants in the political economy of the world outside the home. Material feminists failed to bring about the "socialization of primitive domestic industries," as the Feminist Alliance urged in a 1914 issue of the *Atlantic Monthly,* because they could not interest Americans in their political or social ideals in sufficient numbers to affect the design and manufacture of kitchen utensils.[75] Some of the less radical ideas of domestic science about the efficiency

[72] Christine Frederick, *Selling Mrs. Consumer* (New York: The Business Bourse, 1929), 43–54.

[73] Ibid., 388–94.

[74] Ibid., 3–5.

[75] Daniel S. Smith, "Family Limitation, Sexual Control, and Domestic Feminism in Victorian America," in *Clio's Consciousness Raised: New Perspectives on the History of Women,* ed. Mary Hartman and Lois W. Banner (New York: Harper Colophon Books, 1974), 119–36.

of utensils were embodied in materials such as the Polarware stainless steel pans introduced in 1927, and the better heat transfer of stainless-clad, carbon steel-core cookware introduced in the 1930s.[76] Nonetheless, the original connections that material feminists made between the properties of kitchen utensils and the political implications of the structure of housework failed to penetrate the commercial market, nor, in the end, to affect the domestic routines of American women.

[76] Lifshey, *Housewares Story,* 156–57.

Cookbooks of the 1800s

ELEANOR T. FORDYCE

FTER the Bible and the telephone directory, the cookbook is reported to be the publication most often consulted in the American home (figs. 1 and 2). In fact, due to the continuous demand for them, cookbooks as a group are best sellers ranking second only to the Bible. Not only are the old compilations still highly valued, but there is a constant demand for the newer titles in cooking.

Though the printing of directions for food preparation has been the primary motive for their production since the first colonial "receipt" (meaning "received rules of cookery") books, this has not been their sole purpose, or their sole teaching. Since colonial times, the cookbook has reflected much of the way of life of people in various sections of the country. Some represent progress in experimental cookery and nutritional research; others reflect the type of food available at a particular period of our history. Still others reveal customs. In short, cookbooks are more than guides to food preparation; they provide evidence of the many changes occurring in family life throughout the United States.

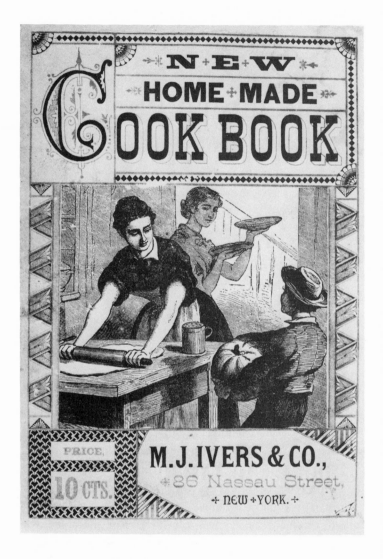

FIG. 1 *Cover,* New Home Made
Cook Book *(New York: M. J. Ivers
and Co., 1882). Courtesy Eleanor
Fordyce.*

Until 1742 when William Parks reprinted the popular English publication *The Compleat Housewife* (written by E. Smith in 1727) in Williamsburg, Virginia, cookbooks had come to this country directly from the English presses; colonial presses more commonly printed legal documents, sermons, catechisms, and almanacs. A book for the household was

FIG. 2 *Frontispiece, "The Queen
of Home," in Mrs. Anne Clark*, The
Ideal Cookery Book *(Chicago: H. J.
Smith and Co., 1889). Courtesy
Eleanor Fordyce.*

therefore a unique business venture. So successful was Parks's
volume that other colonial publishers were inspired to dupli-
cate other European cookery titles. Only four original copies of
The Compleat Housewife now exist; however, the restoration
of Williamsburg inspired the republication of sections of *The
Compleat Housewife* in *The Williamsburg Art of Cookery*.

This newer book includes receipts by Mrs. E. Smith and also by many Virginians. Here are two that Smith wrote in 1727:

Beef À-la-mode

Take a good Buttock of Beef, interlarded with great Lard, roll'd up in [s]avoury Spice, and Sweet-herbs; put in a great Sauce-pan, and cover it close and set it in the oven Over all Night. This is fit to eat cold.

To Make an Apple Tansy

Take three Pippins, slice them round in thin Slices, and fry them with butter, then beat four Eggs, with six Spoonfuls of cream, a little Rose-water, nutmeg, and Sugar, and stir them together, and pour it over the Apples. Let it fry a little, and turn it with a Pye-plate. Garnish with Lemon and Sugar strew'd over it.[1]

In the receipt for beef à la mode, the terms "savoury Spice" and "sweet herbs" most likely indicate no particular spices or herbs; the instructions instead probably mean one can use any spices and herbs on hand. "Great" lard simply translates to a great amount. Apple tansy may be an earlier term for what we would today call an apple crisp or crumble. The combined scarcity and expense of ingredients such as vanilla was often compensated for by the addition of rosewater, a flavoring made by cooking rose petals in water.

Most early American receipts were handed down by word of mouth or in handwritten receipt books. A quaint receipt of the *Plimouth Colony Cookbook* is Indian Pudding: "Take the mornings milk and throw into it as much corn meal as you can hold in the palm of your hand. Let the molasses drip in as you sing 'Nearer My God to Thee,' but sing two verses in cold weather." (Two verses are advised because molasses runs more slowly in cold weather than it does in warm.)[2]

It has been noted that receipts in early cookbooks were usually written in language that applied either to cooking on an

[1] Mrs. E. Smith, *The Compleat Housewife* (Williamsburg, Va.: William Parks, 1742); Helen Claire Bullock, *The Williamsburg Art of Cookery* (Williamsburg, Va.: Colonial Williamsburg, Inc., 1939).

[2] Sally Larkin Evath, ed., *The Plimouth Colony Cookbook* (Plymouth, Mass.: Plymouth Antiquarian Society, 1964), 70. A contemporary example along the same line comes from a newspaper account of a visit by the Rev. Billy Graham to Scotland. The evangelist was surprised at hearing the singing of "Onward Christian Soldiers" from an Edinburgh hotel kitchen. At Graham's query about it, the cook said, "Oh, I always sing that hymn when I boil eggs. Three verses for soft, and five for hard-boiled."

The Kitchen of the Governor's Palace at Williamsburg

FIG. 3 *This frontispiece from* The Williamsburg Art of Cookery *(1939) purports to show the kitchen of the governor's palace at Williamsburg, which, like all kitchens until the nineteenth century, was organized around an open hearth. The cookbook incorporates parts of* The Compleat Housewife *(1727), an English receipt book which was reprinted in Williamsburg in 1742.*

Eleanor T. Fordyce

FIG. 4 *An unusual early advertisement for an "improved cooking stove" made by the foundry of James and Cornell appeared in the anonymous* Experienced American Housekeeper, *published in 1823.*

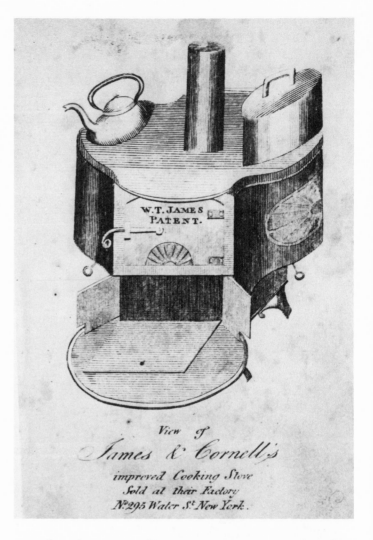

View of

James & Cornell's

improved Cooking Stove
Sold at their Factory
Nº 295 Water Sᵗ New York.

open hearth or to cooking on a cast-iron stove. Foundries began to concentrate on casting such stoves in the 1830s, but the transition from fireplace to stove was not immediate. In the 1841 edition of Catharine Beecher's *American Woman's Home,* a long section was devoted to a discussion of fireplaces; it was not until the 1869 edition that this section was replaced with one on "stoves, furnaces, and chimneys." Moreover, some cooks preferred the taste of meat roasted on the hearth to

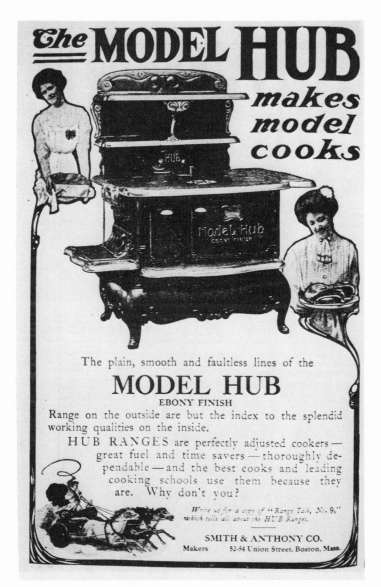

FIG. 5 *Advertisements for stoves
and other kitchen products were a
constant feature in nineteenth-
century cookbooks. Here, in the
1911 edition of Fannie Farmer's
1896 Boston Cooking-School
Cook Book,* the "Hub" line of
cast-iron ranges was promoted
with the imprimatur of the cooking
school movement—a "model"
range for "model cooks."

meat baked in an oven, and in significant ways early cast-iron
stoves were no easier to regulate than open hearth fires; it was
hard to maintain a constant temperature in either (figs. 3–6).
Pre–Civil War cookbooks gave directions for both types of

Eleanor T. Fordyce

FIG. 6 *Cookbooks produced by local women's groups, often reliant on advertising to underwrite the cost of printing, also featured stove advertisements. The back cover of the 1895 edition of* Mother Hubbard's Cupboard, *a volume of recipes collected by the Young Ladies' Society of the First Baptist Church in Rochester, N.Y., displayed the local Sill Stove Work's Sterling range, a stove whose touted "improvements" may have required as much of the housewife's attention as earlier models had. Courtesy Eleanor Fordyce.*

[3] Susan Strasser, *Never Done: A History of American Housework* (New York: Pantheon Books, 1982), 36; Ruth Schwartz Cowan, *More Work for Mother: The Ironies of Household Technology from the Open Hearth to the Microwave* (New York: Basic Books, Inc., 1983), 54–55, 61.

cooking and often recommended interchangeable equipment. Receipts which called for items to be put on the fire or fried could be made on either an open fire or a stove.[3]

After the American Revolution, the ratification of the Constitution, and the acceptance of the Bill of Rights, cookbooks began to reflect the social, economic, political, and intellectual ferment widespread in the last quarter of the eighteenth century. In 1796, Amelia Simmons, "An American orphan," wrote *American Cookery,* thought to be the first printed cookbook prepared by an American. It was the first collection of colonial receipts to be protected by the new copyright act, which became law in 1787, and it was the first cookery title in which the word "American" appeared. Following the trend of the period, the names of many of her receipts were adapted to the idea of the new republic—"Election cake," "Independence cake," "Washington pie"—or reflected Amelia Simmons's apparent concern that the American housewife prepare a bill of fare that would be typical of the new nation, as "Quaker omlet," "Indian slap jack," and "Flannel cake" suggest.[4] More than thirty years later, in 1832, Lydia Maria Child expressed similar nationalistic urgings in the twelfth edition of *The American Frugal Housewife:* "It has become necessary to change the title of this work to the 'American Frugal Housewife,' " Mrs. Child wrote on the copyright page of the volume, "because there is an English work of the same name, not adapted to the wants of this country."[5]

In contrast to Mrs. E. Smith of England, who obviously preferred to remain unknown, Amelia Simmons manifested a spirit of independence by using her first name in connection with her authorship. This too was a sign of the times, and may indicate the progress women were making in their crusade for recognition. In her preface she stated, "This treatise is calculated for the improvement of the rising generation of females in America."[6]

The number and nature of the receipts included in *American Cookery* indicate that a large proportion of the food materials advocated by present-day nutritionists were available in 1796. The homemaker used those things that could be grown in a garden or on a farm, that could be dried or preserved, and that grew wild in the woods. She used cornmeal, whole rye and sometimes whole wheat flours, and brown sugar imported in a loaf; she made her own lard. In receipts of the period, fruits and vegetables and whole cereals were emphasized. However,

[4] Amelia Simmons, *American Cookery* (1796; reprint, Troy, N.Y.: Wright, Goodenow and Stockwell, 1808).

[5] Lydia Maria Child, *The American Frugal Housewife,* 12th ed. (Boston: Carter, Hendee, and Co., 1832), copyright page.

[6] Simmons, *American Cookery.*

neither oranges nor tomatoes were mentioned; oranges were not commonly available, and tomatoes—considered poisonous by many—did not begin to be included in receipts until around 1850. Here are three receipts from *American Cookery:*

To Roast Beef

The general rules are, to have a brisk hot fire, to hang down rather than to spit, to baste with salt and water, and one quarter of an hour to every pound of beef, tho' tender beef will require less, while old tough beef will require more roasting; pricking with a fork will determine you whether done or not; rare done is the healthiest and the taste of this age.

Apple pie

Stew and strain the apples, to every three pints, grate the peal of a fresh lemon, add cinnamon, mace, rose-water and sugar to your taste—and bake in paste No. 3.
Paste No. 3—To any quantity of flour, rub in three fourths of its weight in butter, (twelve eggs to a peck) rub in one third or half, and roll in the rest.

Shrewsbury Cake

One pound butter, three quarters of a pound sugar, a little mace, four eggs mixed and beat with your hand, till very light, put the composition to one pound flour, roll into small cakes—bake with light oven.[7]

Although Miss Simmons's directions were thought to be very meticulous, no doubt the modern cook would have trouble following them. Her measurements were given in terms of pounds, gills, pints, and quarts. Usually, instructions for combining them were vague. One recipe recommended, "Mix all up together with one or two Eggs, Butter, Pepper, Salt etc." Another called for "some" butter, and a "bunch" of sweet herbs, and "a little" salt, all to be placed in a "moderate quantity" of water. In a way, recipes probably served chiefly to jog

[7] Ibid.

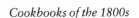

FIG. 7 *A children's book which included recipes,* Six Little Cooks, or Aunt Jane's Cooking Class, *was published in Chicago in 1877. Its frontispiece stressed learning by experience and the example of others. Note that no measuring devices appear among the implements on the table.*

the memory, for many cooking skills, recipes, and notions about the proper amount of ingredients were probably transmitted largely by example (fig. 7).

American Cookery started a vogue for the printing of receipts by Americans, mostly women (fig. 8). About 160 titles appeared in the first half of the nineteenth century, including the 1808 volume *The New England Cookery,* compiled by Lucy Emerson; *A New System of Domestic Cookery,* "By a Lady," in 1807; *The Universal Cook Book* by one Priscilla Homespun, published in 1818; Miss Prudence Smith's *Modern American Cookery* (1831); and the first of domestic adviser

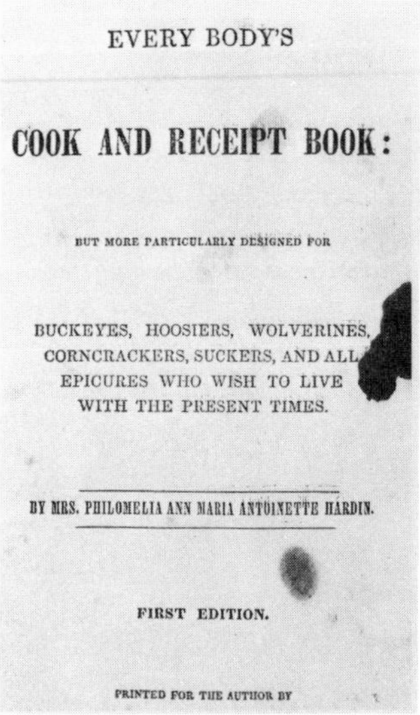

Eleanor T. Fordyce

EVERY BODY'S

COOK AND RECEIPT BOOK:

BUT MORE PARTICULARLY DESIGNED FOR

BUCKEYES, HOOSIERS, WOLVERINES,
CORNCRACKERS, SUCKERS, AND ALL
EPICURES WHO WISH TO LIVE
WITH THE PRESENT TIMES.

BY MRS. PHILOMELIA ANN MARIA ANTOINETTE HARDIN.

FIRST EDITION.

PRINTED FOR THE AUTHOR BY

FIG. 8 Every Body's Cook and
Receipt Book, *published in Cleveland in 1842, is believed to be the
earliest work devoted primarily to
cookery published west of the Ohio
River. The cookbook's title page,
and many of its recipes, articulated
a growing sense of regional identity, beyond the nationalistic under-
tones of many antebellum American cookbooks. Courtesy Eleanor
Fordyce.*

[8] Child, *American Frugal Housewife,* title page.

Miss Eliza Leslie's many books, *Seventy-Five Receipts for
Pastry, Cakes, and Sweetmeats* (1837). *Seventy-Five Receipts*
was an accumulation of recipes which she had learned in Mrs.
Goodfellow's Philadelphia cooking school course—and which
she had habitually copied out for friends until one of her
brothers suggested that she publish them.

The early American cookbook was usually divided into three
parts, with sections on cookery, medicine, and household
hints. It may have been, for some women, their only book. As
population dispersed and transportation remained difficult,
many women who had formerly sought advice from family
members and neighbors suddenly found themselves bereft of it.
With little professional assistance available to homemakers,
the receipt book was used in ministering to the ordinary as well
as the emergency needs of their households. They also, quite
often, provided the philosophical underpinning for a woman
who endeavored to set up and keep a well-ordered home. *The
American Frugal Housewife,* for example, was dedicated "to
those who are not ashamed of economy" and invoked several
aphorisms written by Benjamin Franklin in support of this way
of life on its title page:

> A fat kitchen maketh a lean will.
> Economy is a poor man's revenge.
> Extravagance a rich man's ruin.[8]

To Mrs. Child, the "true economy of housekeeping" was "the
art of the gathering up all the fragments, so that nothing be
lost," an art in which she urged the family's full participation.
"True economy," she wrote, "is a careful treasurer in the
service of benevolence; and where they are united respectability, prosperity and peace will follow." Mrs. Child also
analyzed the plight of those who, living "beyond their income," engaged in a "false and wicked parade":

> it is wrong—morally wrong, so far as the individual is
> concerned; and injurious beyond calculation to the in-

terests of our country. To what are the increasing beggary and discouraged exertions of the present period owing? A multitude of causes have no doubt tended to increase the evil; but the root of the whole matter is the extravagance of all classes of people. We never shall be prosperous till we make pride and vanity yield to the dictates of honesty and prudence! We never shall be free from embarrassment until we cease to be ashamed of industry and economy.[9]

Mrs. Child deliberately wrote her book "for the poor," the young housekeepers of the country who needed but did not possess information about common household practices. "I have said nothing about rich cooking," she wrote, by "rich" probably meaning cooking that depended on greater quantities of butter and refined white sugar or a greater variety of expensive ingredients such as vanilla; "those who can afford to be epicures will find the best of information in the 'Seventy-five Receipts,' " she wrote. "I have attempted to teach how money can be saved, not how it can be enjoyed" (fig. 9).[10]

The American Frugal Housewife included instructions on how to use straw from crops to make bonnets and hats, how to turn the feathers of turkey and geese into fans, how to use eggs to kill bedbugs, how to use skim milk and water to restore certain fabrics, how to keep pumps from freezing, how to clean lamp wicks, how to keep flies off gilt frames (because some kinds of gilt would be removed if one attempted to wash away fly specks), how to smooth sadirons. In this world, even lint from worn-out linen rags and suds from washing clothes and dishes had use. In the chapter "Odd Scraps for the Economical," Mrs. Child listed more than 100 bits of advice for the household. Some, though certainly not all of these, relate to foods:

> Look frequently to the pails, to see that nothing is thrown to the pigs which should have been in the grease-pot.
>
> Look to the grease-pot, and see that nothing is there

FIG. 9 *Many nineteenth-century American cookbooks stressed moderate, if not frugal, living. Their frequent inclusion of money-saving recipes associated, implicitly or explicitly, the excesses of "rich cooking" with the follies of fashion. Not all cookbooks rejected such inclinations, however. Published simultaneously in London and New York,* Entrées and Table Dainties for the Epicure *(1889), featured an American engraving of a dining scene, complete with a well-dressed servant and champagne cooling on the floor, on its cover. Courtesy Eleanor Fordyce.*

[9] Ibid., 5–6.
[10] Ibid., 6.

which might have served to nourish your own family, or a poorer one. . . .

As far as it is possible, have bits of bread eaten up before they become hard. Spread those that are not eaten, and let them dry, to be pounded for puddings, or soaked for brewis. Brewis is made of crusts and dry pieces of bread, soaked a good while in hot milk, mashed up, and salted, and buttered like toast. Above all, do not let crusts accumulate in such quantities that they cannot be used. With proper care, there is no need of losing a particle of bread, even in the hottest weather. . . .

Eggs will keep almost any length of time in lime-water properly prepared. One pint of coarse salt, and one pint of unslacked lime, to a pailful of water. If there be too much lime, it will eat the shells from the eggs; and if there be a single egg cracked, it will spoil the whole. They should be covered with lime-water, and kept in a cold place. The yolk becomes slightly red; but I have seen eggs, thus kept, perfectly sweet and fresh at the end of three years. The cheapest time to lay down eggs, is early in spring, and the middle and last of September. It is bad economy to buy eggs by the dozen, as you want them. . . .

Have all the good bits of vegetables and meat collected after dinner, and minced before they are set away; that they may be in readiness to make a little savoury mince meat for supper or breakfast. Take the skins off your potatoes before they grow cold.[11]

Such economies had been stressed just as strongly earlier, as this receipt for "Common Pancakes" from the 1817 edition of *A New System of Domestic Cookery* shows:

Make a light batter of eggs, flour and milk. Fry in a small pan, in hot dripping or lard. Salt or nutmeg and ginger, may be added. Sugar and lemon should be served to eat with them. Or, when eggs are scarce, make the batter with

[11] Ibid., 8, 11, 17.

flour, and small beer, ginger, &c. or clean snow, with flour, and a very little milk, will serve as well as egg.[12]

American cookbooks also frequently contained suggestions for the "care of food." *A New System of Domestic Cookery* advised cooks that "vegetables will keep best on a stone floor; if air is excluded. Meat in a cold dry place. Sugar and sweetmeats require a dry place; so does salt. Candles cold but not damp. Dried meats, hams etc, the same. All sorts of seeds for puddings, . . . rice etc should be close covered, to preserve from insects, but that will not prevent it, if kept long."[13] In *The Experienced American Housekeeper, or Domestic Cookery* of 1823, these suggestions are copied almost word for word, as they also are in the 1841 *Temperance Cook Book*. It has been noted that throughout the nineteenth century, home preserving of vegetables other than by drying or storing in root cellars was not common, because most other methods of preserving foods were not effective; in fact, home canning probably was not widespread until the twentieth century, when machines were invented that could make glass jars, and when the government promoted home canning during the the First World War.[14]

In these cookbooks from the earlier part of the nineteenth century, at least as much space was devoted to medicine as was given to food. In *The New England Economical Housekeeper* of 1845 there appeared recipes for and short treatises on foods of supposed medicinal value, among them "Dyspepsia Bread" (made of unbolted wheat meal, "soft . . . but not hot" water, yeast, and "molasses, or not, as may suit the taste"), as well as "Carrot Pie" and "Ripe Bread":

Ripe Bread

Bread made of wheat flour, when taken from the oven, is unprepared for the stomach. It should go through a change, or ripen, before it is eaten. It not only has more nutriment but imparts a greater degree of cheerfulness. He that eats old ripe bread will have a greater flow of animal spirits than he would were he to eat unripe bread.[15]

[12] A Lady [Maria Eliza Ketelby Rundell], *A New System of Domestic Cookery* (1807; reprint, New York: Robert McDermut, 1817).

[13] Ibid.

[14] *The Experienced American Housekeeper, or Domestic Cookery* (New York: Johnstone and Van Norden, 1823); Strasser, *Never Done*, 20–22.

[15] Mrs. E. A. Howland, *The New England Economical Housekeeper* (Montpelier, Vt.: E. P. Walton and Sons, 1845), 13.

One-third of *The New Family Book, or Ladies' Indispensable Companion and Housekeepers' Guide* of 1854 discussed medical "recipes":

MEDICINES: Never give medicine to a very young child. Many have thus lost darling children. It will, if not murdered, be permanently injured. It cries often on account of tight clothes or the pricking of pins. If medicine must be given at all, give it to the nurse. . . .

RECIPE FOR PUTRID SORE THROAT: Mix one gill of strong apple vinegar, one table-spoonful of common salt, one table-spoonful of drained honey and a half pod of red pepper together, boil them to a proper consistency, then pour it into half pint of strong sage tea, take a tea-spoonful occasionally and it will be found an infallible cure. . . .

TO TAKE DOWN SWELLING: White beans merely stewed soft, and put in thin muslin bags. A poultice of the roots of Yellow Water Lily is very powerful in drawing tumors to a head. . . .

SICK HEADACHE: Take a tea-spoonful of powdered charcoal in molasses every morning, and wash it down with a little tea; or, Drink half a glass of raw rum or gin, and drink freely of mayweed tea. . . .

EAR-ACHE: Roast a piece of lean mutton, squeeze out the juice and drop it into the ear as hot as it can be borne; or, Roast an onion, and put it into the ear, as hot as it can be borne.[16]

Etiquette for ladies and gentlemen also was not overlooked in these volumes. *The New Family Book* provided advice on deportment and clothing similar in spirit to Mrs. Child's recommendations about the role of moderation in the household:

Cleanliness, absolute purity of person, is the first requisite in the appearance of a gentleman or lady. Not only should the face and the hands be kept clean, but the whole skin should be subject to frequent ablutions. Better wear coarse

[16] *The New Family Book, or Ladies' Indispensable Companion and Housekeepers' Guide* (New York: E. Hutchinson, 1854).

clothes with a clean skin, than silk stockings drawn over dirty feet. Let the whole skin be kept pure and sweet, the teeth and nails and hair, clean: and the last two of medium length, and naturally cut. Nothing deforms a man more than a hair-cutting, and unnatural deformity in wearing it. Abstain from all eccentricities. Take a medium between nature and fashion, which is perhaps the best rule in regard to dress and appearance that can be given.[17]

In the middle of the century, a new form of editorship occurred—the custom of compiling receipts contributed by the members of women's organizations. New organizations appeared that were devoted exclusively to women's interests, and some of the cookery literature published at this time sprung directly from and in behalf of such groups. For some of the more politically inclined groups, cookbooks were used not only to raise money but to promote their objectives. *The Woman's Suffrage Cook Book* appeared at that time; *The Temperance Cook Book,* written by "A Lady," appeared slightly earlier, in 1841 (fig. 10). The title page of the latter volume featured a different title—*Total Abstinence Cookery*—and its preface stated that the sole reason for publishing the book was "to furnish another aid to the Temperance Reformation."

> The error of mixing intoxicating liquors in almost every article of cookery, has too long been countenanced by those who have charge of families; and every friend of temperance must most sincerely deplore the fact, that in almost every book that has heretofore been published for a housekeeper's assistant, this pernicious evil has been encouraged and supported. . . . it is here affirmed without fear of successful contradiction, that the receipts herein given, if faithfully observed, will enable the housekeeper to furnish her family with food more agreeable to the taste . . . than any other work of the kind ever offered to the public. It is therefore, hoped, that it will be adopted by

FIG. 10 *The central image of the well on the cover of the 1841* Temperance Cook Book *associated the volume with the movement's second identity—the "cold water crusade" against the consumption of spiritous liquors. Courtesy Eleanor Fordyce.*

[17] Ibid.

FIG. 11 *Journalist C. W. Gesner once complained in an 1866 issue of* Harper's New Monthly Magazine, *"We cry for pie when we are infants. Pie in countless varieties waits upon us through life. Pie kills us finally." That nineteenth-century Americans were apparently enamored of pies may account for the fact that images of women cooking pies were ubiquitous in American cookbooks. This woman was shown on the cover of* Cooking Recipes, Tested and Proved, *a volume produced in Pittsfield, Maine, by the ladies' organization of the local Universalist Church for its 1889 Universalist Fair. Courtesy Eleanor Fordyce.*

COOKING RECIPES
TESTED AND PROVED

COMPILED FOR
UNIVERSALIST FAIR,
By The U. L. S. A. Society.

all who are the true friends of the great Temperance Reform.[18]

Women's groups with no obvious political motivation often published cookbooks after 1850 solely to raise funds. In 1880, the Young Ladies Society of the First Baptist Church in Rochester, New York, published *Mother Hubbard's Cupboard;* the Ladies' Aid Society of the Methodist Episcopal Church of Charmont, New York, published its second edition of *Tried and True Receipes* in 1897. In the same year, the

[18] Mrs. Hattie A. Burr, ed., *The Woman's Suffrage Cook Book* (Boston: Hattie A. Burr, 1886); A Lady, *The Temperance Cook Book* (Philadelphia: Eugene Commiskey, 1841), 3–4.

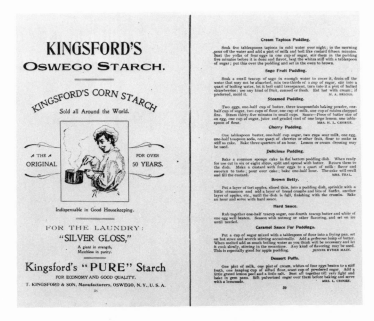

FIG. 12 *The Ladies' Aid Society of the Charmont, N.Y., Methodist Episcopal Church clearly relied on advertisements from nearby manufacturers to help finance the second edition of its* Tried and True Receipts, *published in 1897. It is interesting to note that, although corn starch was a short cut for the long steaming or baking which puddings usually required, none of the pudding recipes on the page facing the Kingsford's Corn Starch advertisement calls for it. Courtesy Eleanor Fordyce.*

Thought and Work Club of Salem, Massachusetts, published *The Up-to-Date Cook Book*. These represent a very small percentage of volumes published by such women's organizations in the nineteenth century; the tradition of such publishing has been vigorously maintained in the twentieth century (figs. 11–15).

For other groups, some not restricted to women, the major motivation for publishing cookbooks was to promulgate certain theories about the relation of food to health, income, and civilization. Dr. Albert J. Bellows dedicated his 1883 edition of *The Philosophy of Eating* to "the five thousand ladies who, from 1838 to 1858, attended my lectures on physiology, chemistry, and hygiene," and he went on to deplore the general ignorance of the population about the "laws of nature" and what they mandate about the preparation of food:

they give their pigs the food which their children need to develop muscle and brain, and give their children what their pigs need to develop fat. For example, the farmer

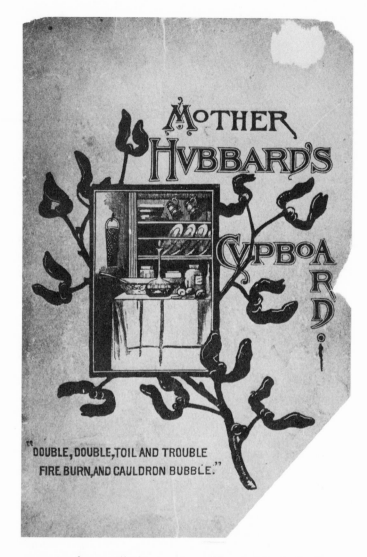

FIG. 13 *Cover,* Mother Hubbard's Cupboard: Recipes Collected by the Young Ladies Society, First Baptist Church, Rochester, New York *(1880; reprint, Rochester, N.Y.: Scrantom, Wetmore and Co., 1895). Courtesy Eleanor Fordyce.*

separates from milk the muscle-making and brain-feeding nitrates and phosphates, and gives them to his pigs in the form of buttermilk, while the fattening carbohydrates he gives to his children in butter. . . . Cheese, which contains the concentrated nutriment of milk, is seldom seen on our tables, while butter, which contains not a particle of food for brain or muscle, is on every table at all times of day.[19]

[19] Albert J. Bellows, M.D., *The Philosophy of Eating,* 14th ed. (Boston: Houghton, Mifflin and Co., 1883), 4.

FIG. 14 *The advertisements that helped fund Grace A. Oliver's* Up-to-Date Cook Book *(1897), undertaken by the Salem, Mass., Thought and Work Club, stressed the growing concern about having the "right things" to cook with. The quickening interest in modernity is also suggested by this woman's kitchen, which includes a hot water tank. Courtesy Eleanor Fordyce.*

Nearly thirty years earlier, the hydrotherapist Dr. Russell T. Trall argued for making "the subject of diet" a standard course "in all our seminaries of learning" in *The New Hydropathic Cook-Book:*

> Whether humanity must become good in order to be happy, or must first become happy in order to be good, is a very pretty metaphysical problem for discussion; but, pending its solution, I will undertake to say, that human beings will never be, in an exalted sense, either good or happy, until they shall have obtained that harmonious and healthful play of all the bodily and mental functions which constitute "peace within;" and that such a consummation can never be realized until a thorough and radical reform is effected in the eating habits of the civilized people.[20]

The introduction and growth of the home economics movement affected cookbooks greatly during the nineteenth century. In *The American Frugal Housewife* in 1829, Lydia Maria Child had recommended that girls train in their mothers' duties

[20] R. T. Trall, *The New Hydropathic Cook-Book* (New York: Fowlers and Wells, 1854), iv–v.

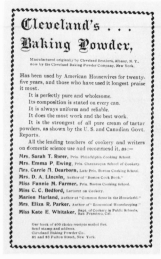

FIG. 15 *Advertisers of kitchen
goods and foodstuffs made liberal
use of endorsements from cooking
school principals and authors of
advice books on the new "domestic
science." Inside front cover in*
Up-to-Date Cook Book. *Courtesy
Eleanor Fordyce.*

[21] Strasser, *Never Done,* 189–
91, 203.
[22] Catharine Beecher, *A Treatise
on Domestic Economy* (1841;
reprint, New York: Harper and
Brothers, 1858), 65.
[23] Strasser, *Never Done,* 203.

and responsibilities for several years, but by the time Catharine Beecher wrote *Miss Beecher's Domestic Receipt Book* in 1842, apprenticeship in the home was not considered adequate.[21] Advocating school-based instruction in home economics, Beecher wrote in her 1841 *Treatise on Domestic Economy* (a companion volume to the *Receipt Book*), "As a general fact, young ladies *will not* be taught these things in any other way. In reply to the thousand-times-repeated remark, that girls must be taught their domestic duties by their mothers, at home, it may be inquired, in the first place, What proportion of mothers are qualified to teach a *proper* and *complete* system of Domestic Economy?"[22]

Beecher wrote at a time when education for women was being promoted with considerable success as part of an over-arching concern with increasing the knowledge and competency of society as a whole. Within several decades, home economics training became a reality; the first college instruction in the area was introduced at Iowa State College in 1872.[23] *Miss Beecher's Domestic Receipt Book* was a very significant contribution to the literature of cookery. It was the first foods laboratory manual to be used as a textbook, the first to be accepted as such by a state department of education, and the volume that set a precedent for later publications to be used in home economics instruction.

The cooking school movement, organized at about the same time, resulted in another trend of cookery publications. These were products of various schools organized in Boston, New York, and Philadelphia. Mrs. D. A. Lincoln's *Boston School Kitchen Text-Book,* published in 1887; Maria Parloa's *New Cook Book,* published in Boston in 1881; and Mrs. Sarah T. Rorer's 1886 *New Cook Book* are examples (fig. 16). *The Boston Cooking-School Cook Book,* often known simply as *The Fannie Farmer Cook Book,* was first published in 1896. Like the treatises on domestic economy, these volumes made a definite contribution to food courses in the newly organized

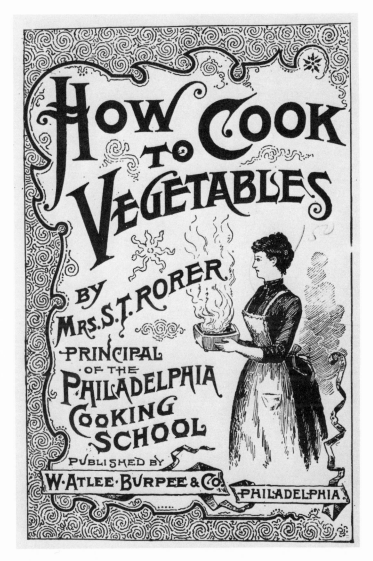

home economics departments of colleges and universities, where the emphasis was on food preparation as a science. Measurements and the tools with which they were made became more exact. Concern about imprecise measurements had been voiced at least as early as 1846, when Catharine Beecher

Eleanor T. Fordyce

FIG. 17 *Some cooking school principals, such as Mary J. Lincoln of the Boston Cooking School, even began to produce products that embodied the theories of their movement. Then secretary of her own baking powder company and culinary editor of* American Kitchen *magazine, Mrs. Lincoln claimed that her powder was "a pure food product, prepared with skill and accuracy after a well tested formula, and needing no other endorsement as to its purity than my guarantee on every label, and only a fair trial by intelligent house-keepers, to prove its merit." Cover of* Mrs. Lincoln's Baking Powder Company Cook Book *(Boston: Mrs. Lincoln's Baking Powder Co., 1899). Courtesy Eleanor Fordyce.*

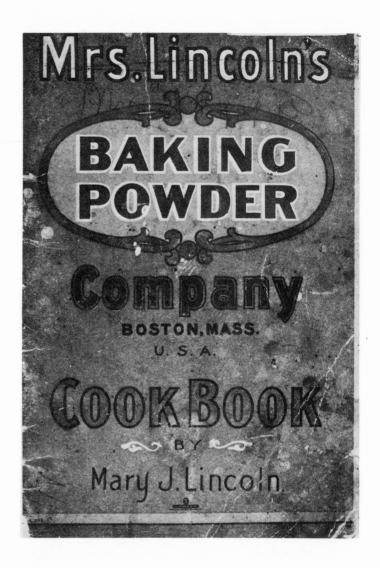

[24] Catharine Beecher, *Miss Beecher's Domestic Receipt Book,* 5th ed. (New York: Harper and Brothers, 1846), 277.

sympathized with the "discouraged housekeeper" who could not cope with "indefinite instructions" such as " 'Take a *pinch* of this, and a *little* of that, and *considerable* of the other, and cook them till they are done *about right*.' "[24] By the 1870s, cookbook authors began to offer tables to translate from terms such as "pinch," or butter "the size of a walnut." In a cookbook prepared in part to promote her own baking powder company, Mrs. Lincoln translated a pinch of salt as one-eighth of a teaspoon and a "shake" of pepper as one-quarter square inch. "By the cooking school measure of level teaspoons, —that is, —teaspoons cut off with a knife, so the powder is just on a line with the edge of the spoon, —each teaspoon of the old measure would be equal to two and possibly a trifle more of the new. This must be kept strictly in mind in following these recipes" (fig. 17).[25] As Fannie Farmer noted in *The Boston Cooking-School Cook Book,* "Correct measurements are absolutely necessary to insure the best results. Good judgment, with experience, has taught some to measure by sight; but the majority need definite guides" (figs. 18 and 19).[26]

The cooking school cookbooks also reflect the tendency of the society at large to professionalize, and to disperse the growing body of "scientific" knowledge about nutrition and health. Mrs. D. A. Lincoln's preface to her *Boston School Kitchen Text-Book* illustrates these preoccupations:

Cooking cannot be well done by guess-work. There is a right way and a wrong way, and the right way is usually the easier. To show the right way and reasons for it has been the endeavor in preparing these lessons. It can not be expected to make professional cooks in twenty lessons. But it is confidently believed that if school girls will master the elementary principles which these lessons illustrate, they can, with practice at home, acquire a skill sufficient to do all that is necessary in plain family living.[27]

Many of the cooking schools organized classes for different kinds of cooks. Cooking schools were initiated by urban reformers on behalf of working women, but some, such as Juliet Corson's New York Cooking School, offered classes for wealthy women, mission-school students, and hired cooks or workers' wives.[28] In 1890, Mrs. Mary Hinman Abel's *Practical Sanitary and Economic Cooking Adapted to Persons of Mod-*

[25] Mary J. Lincoln [Mrs. D. A. Lincoln], *Mrs. Lincoln's Baking Powder Company* (Boston: Mrs. Lincoln's Baking Powder Co., 1899), inside front cover.
[26] Fannie Merritt Farmer, *The Boston Cooking-School Cook Book* (1896; rev. ed., Boston: Little, Brown, and Co., 1911), 25.
[27] Mrs. D. A. Lincoln [Mary Johnson Bailey Lincoln], *Boston School Kitchen Text-Book* (Boston: Roberts Bros., 1888, vii–viii.
[28] Strasser, *Never Done,* 204.

Eleanor T. Fordyce

FIGS. 18 and 19 *Some of the later editions of Fannie Farmer's* Boston Cooking-School Cook Book, *such as this 1911 volume, featured photographs of the kitchen measuring and food processing utensils which by then were considered absolutely essential to successful cooking. Note also the "sanitary" enamel sauce and frying pans.*

erate and Small Means, offered "bills of fare" for families of six in three income classes (fig. 20). Mrs. Abel, the wife of a professor of pharmacology, had been much impressed with the "people's kitchens" she had seen during a trip to Germany with her husband. Her book received first prize in an essay contest sponsored by Rochester, New York, lens manufacturer Henry Lomb on behalf of the American Public Health Association, a group organized in 1872 for "the amelioration of sickness and suffering, and the prolongation of human life." With Massachusetts Institute of Technology sanitary chemist Ellen

BILLS OF FARE, CLASS I.

For family of six, average price 78 cents per day, or 13 cents per person.

SATURDAY, MAY.

Breakfast.
Flour Pancakes,
(p. 103) with Sugar Syrup.
Coffee.

Dinner.
Bread Soup (p. 20).
Beefneck Stew
Noodles (p. 90).
Swelled Rice Pudding (p. 107).

Supper.

Browned Flour Soup, with Fried Bread (p. 121).
Toast and Cheese (page 62, No. 1).

	Proteids. oz.	Fats. oz.	Carbo-hydrates. oz.	Cost in Cents.
½ lb. Rice	.64	.08	6.12	4
1 lb. Sugar	....	....	15.42	7
¾ lb. Fat Cheese	3.00	3.48	.24	11¼
2 qts. Skim Milk	2.12	.48	3.30	8
2 lb. Flour	3.84	.48	22.88	6
½ qt. Whole Milk	.58	.62	.83	3½
2 Eggs	.34	.32	....	3
2½ lbs. Beef neck	8.40	2.20	....	20
⅜ lb. Suet	....	5.88	....	3
⅛ lb. Coffee	....	....	....	3⅖
3½ lbs. Bread	3.36	.28	29.06	8 1/20
Total	22.28	13.82	77.85	77⅕
Required	19.19	12.42	78.03	78

FIG. 20 *Progressive urban reformers also issued cookbooks to guide working women and the poor toward inexpensive but "nutritional" foods. Mary Hinman Abel's* Practical Sanitary and Economic Cooking Adapted to Persons of Moderate and Small Means, *which included bills of fare for people in three income "classes," won the 1890 American Public Health Association's essay contest even though, by today's standards, its menus provide far from a balanced diet.*

Richards, Abel established the New England Kitchen in Boston in 1890. A public kitchen designed to teach American workers to eat more scientifically, the New England Kitchen was to demonstrate the connection between proper eating and sobriety by acting as an alternative to the saloon. Based on the premise that inadequate diet was hastening the physical and moral ruination of Americans, Abel's volume shared the spirit of American Progressivism, and the New England Kitchen spawned similar public kitchens in New York and in Chicago, at Hull House (fig. 21).[29]

Although the first American newspaper was printed in 1704, the printing of receipts within magazines and newspapers did not become popular until the latter half of the nineteenth century. *Peterson's Ladies' National Magazine* contained the

29 Mary Hinman Abel, *Practical Sanitary and Economic Cooking Adapted to Persons of Moderate and Small Means* (Rochester, N.Y.: American Public Health Association, 1890); Harvey Levenstein, "The New England Kitchen and the Origins of Modern American Eating Habits," *American Quarterly* 32, no. 4 (Fall 1980): 371–74, 377–78.

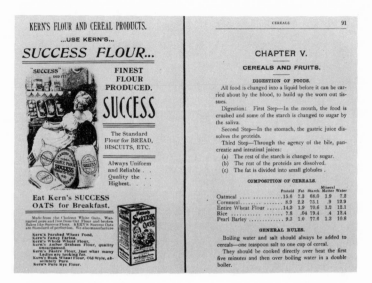

FIG. 21 *In step with progressive reform, some settlement houses published cookbooks. This spread, which reflects the influence of domestic science, is from* The Way to a Man's Heart: Under the Auspices of "The Settlement," *published in Milwaukee in 1901. Courtesy Eleanor Fordyce.*

column "Our New Cook Book" in 1868; *The Ladies' Home Journal* also contained a cooking column in the last years of the century, as did *The Ladies Home Companion, Conkey's Home Journal,* and *The Today Book.* Fannie Farmer wrote monthly food columns in *The Woman's Home Companion* from 1905 to 1915.

When goods and services became more readily available and communications expanded, the "receipt book" was revised. First, changes in family size affected how recipes were written. After 1870 new receipts were written for an average family of four. In 1860, when Miss Beecher's recipe book was popular, ten to twelve was regarded as the "average" number in a healthy family.

The connection between cookery and the state of civilization is one that has been asserted more or less continually over the history of the cookbook. In 1896, Fannie Farmer observed, "Progress in civilization has been accompanied by progress in cookery,"[30] a sentiment that had been voiced by Owen Meredith more than thirty years earlier:

[30] Farmer, *Boston Cooking-School Cook Book,* 25.

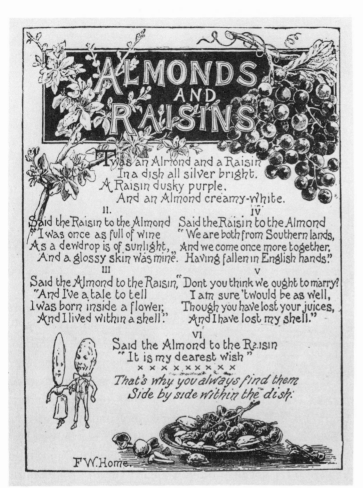

FIG. 22 *Illustration from
Mrs. Grace Townsend,* The
Favorite Cook Book: A Complete
Culinary Encyclopedia *(Chicago:
W. B. Conkey Co., 1894). Courtesy
Eleanor Fordyce.*

We may live without poetry, music, and art;
We may live without conscience and live without heart;
We may live without friends, we may live without books;
But civilized man cannot live without cooks.[31]

31 Owen Meredith [Edward
George Earle Lytton Bulwer-
Lytton], *Lucile* (1860; reprint,
St. Petersburg: S. Dufour, 1866),
pt. 1, canto 2, st. 19.

Rituals of Dining

TABLE MANNERS IN VICTORIAN AMERICA

JOHN F. KASSON

 century ago, at a meeting of the Anthropological Society of Washington, a speaker attempted to bring the perspective of his discipline to the study of table manners. Surveying other cultures and ages briefly, he smugly declared: "Brutes feed. The best barbarian only eats. Only the cultured man can dine. Dining is no longer a meal, but an institution" (fig. 1).[1] In all its ethnocentric and self-congratulatory aspects, this statement expressed both the anthropological and the conventional wisdom of late nineteenth-century America. It also represents the kind of analysis I wish to avoid.

The subject of table manners still exerts a fascination among modern anthropologists and other social scientists (including a few wayward cultural historians), but they are wary of facile claims of evolutionary cultural progress. Instead, they emphasize that eating is a ritual activity, invested with special meaning, in all cultures. Such a primary bodily activity, with all its attendant vulnerability, requires "protective symbolic cover-

[1] Garrick Mallery, "Manners and Meals," *The American Anthropologist* 1 (July 1888): 195. Mallery notes that this article was based upon a more extended paper presented before the society in April 1886.

FIG. 1 *The Harrison Grey Fiske dinner, New York, 1900. Courtesy The Byron Collection, Museum of the City of New York.*

ing."[2] The distinctive ways in which different peoples eat express their attitudes toward their physical bodies, their social relationships, and their sense of the larger cultural order. In uncovering those attitudes, we may reveal aspects of a culture that are in other respects less obvious. At the same time we must not claim too much. No single ritual or set of rituals, particularly in a pluralistic culture such as that of nineteenth-century America, can provide a skeleton key that unlocks the innermost meanings of a people. Instead, what secular as well as religious rituals characteristically do is to mediate among ambiguous and frequently contending realms of value. They allow participants to negotiate among various aspects of their experience and often to articulate in heightened form elements that are to some degree embattled or suppressed in everyday life.[3]

[2] Carl D. Schneider, *Shame, Exposure, and Privacy* (Boston: Beacon Press, 1977), 66–67.

[3] See Roland A. Delattre, "The Rituals of Humanity and the Rhythms of Reality," in *Prospects: An Annual of American Cultural Studies*, ed. Jack Salzman (New York: Burt Franklin, 1980), 5:35–49.

John F. Kasson

FIG. 2 *From Thomas Fella,* A Book of Divers Devices *(ca. 1585–1622). Courtesy The Folger Shakespeare Library, Washington, D.C.*

Anyone contemplating the history of table manners cannot help being struck by the extraordinary transformation in notions of propriety and refinement from the late Middle Ages to the late nineteenth century. Although the twentieth century has witnessed a growing informality in many respects, our attitudes are still far closer to our ancestors' of the past century than to those who came before.

Consider, for example, the courtly manners of the late Middle Ages (fig. 2). Although medieval courtiers sneered at the table manners of peasants, by later standards they themselves revealed astonishing crudity in their display of bodily processes and mutual contact in dining. Feudal lords owned opulent knives and spoons and other table decorations, but they simply felt no need for the refined practices or proliferation of utensils of later centuries. Not only did they eat with their hands, drink their soup, and lift dishes to their mouths; they also dipped their fingers freely into common bowls and drank from a common goblet. Often two diners would eat from the same board. The courtesy books of the day offered advice that in later periods would be regarded as too elementary even for children (and sometimes too indelicate to mention at all): don't place half-eaten food in the serving dish; don't blow your nose on the tablecloth (use your fingers instead); don't spit on the table but underneath it, and the like.[4]

The sixteenth-century Dutch painter Jörg Ratgeb depicted the Last Supper conducted according to the prevailing standards of etiquette of his day, with one apostle turning from the table to blow his nose on his fingers, another drinking from a wine bottle, and the rest in various postures of repose that would have been startlingly rude to later generations (fig. 3).[5]

Erasmus's enormously popular book on the subject, *De civilitate morum puerilium* (On Good Manners for Boys), which first appeared in 1526, represented a modest tightening of standards, but certainly not a radical departure: "It is rude to offer someone what you have half eaten yourself . . . just as it is disgusting to spit out chewed food and put it on your plate," Erasmus advised readers. "If you happen to have eaten something that cannot be swallowed, you should discreetly turn away and toss it somewhere."[6]

Beginning in the sixteenth century and continuing through the nineteenth, however, western Europe saw an extraordinary elaboration in table manners, first among the nobility and then among the middle classes. Individual plates and goblets replaced communal ones, and the use of individual forks gradually superseded fingers in polite society and narrowed the scope

[4] Norbert Elias, *The History of Manners: The Civilizing Process,* trans. Edmund Jephcott (New York: Urizen Books, 1978), 1:67.

[5] Bernard Rudofsky (*Now I Lay Me Down to Eat* [Garden City, N.Y.: Anchor Books, 1980]) observes that the sleeping St. John on Jesus' bosom had a long iconographic tradition—and hence should not be mistaken as normal practice for a guest, even in the sixteenth century.

[6] Desiderius Erasmus, "On Good Manners for Boys," trans. Brian McGregor, in *Literary and Educational Writings*, vol. 25 of *Collected Works of Erasmus*, ed. J. K. Sowards (Toronto: University of Toronto Press, 1985), 283; Elias, *History of Manners*, 1:57.

John F. Kasson

of the knife. Diners confronted a proliferating array of specialized utensils and rules for their use. Dining no longer took place in a vast kitchen or hall, but in its own distinct room, apart from the butchering, cooking, and, on the European continent, even the carving of the meat.

According to the great German sociologist Norbert Elias (from whom I have drawn these examples), such developments are by no means isolated curiosities. Quite the contrary, they reflect the growing demands associated with the rise of a more complex, differentiated, interdependent society and the modern state. Increasingly, adults were expected and their children taught to discipline all their appetites and desires, loves and hates, and the manifold gestures expressing them. Not just eating but a whole range of intimate activities—coughing, spitting, nose blowing, scratching, breaking wind, urinating, defecating, undressing, sleeping, copulating, inflicting bodily pain on animals and other human beings—all fell under the sway of rising standards of shame, delicacy, and self-control. As the state assumed a monopoly over physical power and violence, individuals were expected to cultivate reserve and mutual consideration in their dealings. Human emotions and behavior were divided into aspects that might appropriately be displayed in public and others, especially sexuality, that had to be kept private. This split, as Elias emphasizes, has enormous implications for the formation of modern personality, with its internalization of prohibitions, its sensitivity to shame and embarrassment, its highly sensitive "conscience."[7]

Although these stricter standards of self-control originated in the court, the concern with shame and delicacy came to characterize, above all, that great social pyramid, the bourgeoisie, from its apex in manufacturers, merchants, and influential professionals down to its broad base in small shopkeepers and clerks, whose anxious attempts at control reached a height in the Western industrial democracies in the nineteenth century.[8] This transformation was especially striking in the United States, the most thoroughly bourgeois of all societies in the nineteenth century.

The cultivation of etiquette is not usually considered among the history of American conservative social reforms in the nineteenth century. Nonetheless, etiquette writers and other apostles of civility saw themselves battling for far bigger stakes than how best to eat asparagus. Their enterprise must be viewed within the larger concern of how to establish order and authority in a restless, highly mobile, rapidly urbanizing and industrializing democracy. Charges of rudeness frequently expressed deeper fears of licentiousness and riot. The chaotic reception after Andrew Jackson's inauguration in 1829 offers a case in point. According to one horrified account, "a rabble, a mob of boys, negroes, women, children, scrambling, fighting,

[7] Here and in several other passages in this essay, I borrow from my language in "Civility and Rudeness: Urban Etiquette and the Bourgeois Social Order in Nineteenth-Century America," *Prospects* (Cambridge: Cambridge University Press, 1984), 9:143–67.

[8] On the nineteenth-century bourgeoisie, and the attendant problems of definition, see Peter Gay, *The Bourgeois Experience: Victoria to Freud*, vol. 1 of *Education of the Senses* (New York: Oxford University Press, 1984), 17–31, 469–76.

romping," swept into the White House, elbowed dignitaries aside, and almost trampled the president himself. In its wake the "mob" left fainting ladies and men with bloody noses, carpets and chairs smeared with muddy footprints, and several thousand dollars' worth of broken glassware and china.[9] The insolence of an egalitarian order, if unchecked, apparently knew no bounds.

The gibes by contemporary European travelers about American bumptiousness and vulgarity, such as Frances Trollope's notorious *Domestic Manners of the Americans* (1832), rankled domestic readers because, however overdrawn, they could not be easily dismissed. American assertions of social equality, many foreign visitors believed, simply fomented a culture of coarse familiarity and rudeness, particularly among the working classes. As early as 1795, a disillusioned immigrant to America returned to his native England, complaining that "the lower classes will return rude and impertinent answers to questions couched in the most civil terms and will insult a person that bears the appearance of a gentleman, on purpose to shew how much they consider themselves on an equality with him. Civility cannot be purchased from them on any terms; they seem to think that it is incompatible with freedom."[10] Four decades later, Mrs. Trollope claimed that slavery itself appeared "far less injurious to the manners and morals of the [American] people than the fallacious ideas of equality, which are so fondly cherished by the working classes of the white population in America." Servility, she came perilously close to asserting, was essential for civility.[11]

Etiquette advisers gave a divided response to their European critics. Although they avoided the bluntly antidemocratic swipes of Mrs. Trollope and other foreign travelers and denied that their countrymen were uniquely vulgar, they frequently acknowledged the special need for a culture of civility and an established code of manners in this fluid, pluralistic, and often aggressively egalitarian society. Most Americans, one etiquette adviser conceded in 1857, appeared to "regard *Rudeness* and

[9] Letter from Margaret Bayard Smith to her sister Mrs. Andrew Kirkpatrick, Washington, 11 March 1829, in Margaret Bayard Smith, *The First Forty Years of Washington Society,* ed. Gaillard Hunt (New York: Charles Scribner's Sons, 1906), 295–97.

[10] Isaac Weld, Jr., *Travels through the States of North America* (London: John Stockdale, 1800), 37.

[11] Frances Trollope, *Domestic Manners of the Americans,* ed. Donald Smalley (1832; reprint, New York: Vintage Books, 1960), 186.

[12] [Margaret Cockburn Conkling], *The American Gentleman's Guide to Politeness and Fashion* (New York: Derby and Jackson, 1857), 330.

Republicanism as synonymous terms."[12] It was not that
rudeness and vulgarity were absent abroad, another writer observed; but Europe's stratified class structure kept the "rough
and unwashed" at a social and often physical distance from the
affluent. Snug in a first-class railway car, a European traveler
could regard the third-class occupants with "their unkempt
hair, botched and greasy suits, rude manners, and coarse ver-
nacular" as picturesque elements of the social scene. In the
United States, by contrast, where the two classes mingled
promiscuously on trains, in hotels, and in society at large, no
such detachment was possible. Therefore, he concluded fastidi-
ously, "Universal cleanliness and good manners are essential to
democracy."[13]

According to this argument, then, exemplary demonstrations of civility and self-restraint were immensely more important in the American metropolis than in the European
manor. Such demonstrations, etiquette advisers believed,
would ineluctably move others toward similar conduct. Writers adapted, transformed, and generalized the older traditions
of English and continental courtesy books to fit American re-
quirements. The social rituals they prescribed simultaneously
offered a means for social mobility and for social discipline.
Seeking to avoid overt conflict, apostles of civility redefined
potential issues of class and social grievance to matters of social
propriety and "good taste" and turned them back upon the
individual. American advisers frequently argued that etiquette
was to social interchange what civil laws were to society as
a whole. Such analogies served their cause well. Consider the
following passage that moves nimbly from society to "good
society" and reminds prospective members, particularly the
nouveaux riches, that if they fail to observe society's laws, their
punishment will be both swift and just:

A nation is a number of people associated together for
common purposes, and no one questions the right of those
people to make laws for themselves; society is also an

[13] [Robert Tomes], *The Bazar
Book of Decorum* (New York:
Harper and Brothers, 1870), 13.

organized association, and has a perfect right to make laws which shall be binding upon all of its members. Now, what are called the rules of politeness are nothing more than the customs or laws of good society; and no one, however fine his education, or however great his wealth, power, or fame, should feel himself wronged in the least if this society refuses him admission until he has made himself fully acquainted with its laws.[14]

Nonetheless, if etiquette manuals had spoken only to jealous guardians of the gates of polite society, they would have sold far less widely than they did. According to the avowedly incomplete enumeration by Arthur M. Schlesinger, "aside from frequent revisions and new editions, twenty-eight different manuals appeared in the 1830's, thirty-six in the 1840's and thirty-eight more in the 1850's—an average of over three new ones annually in the pre–Civil War decades." In the period from 1870 to World War One, he reported, the flow of volumes rose to a rate of five or six a year, "probably involving far larger editions."[15] Even though Schlesinger's definition of an etiquette manual was a generous one, embracing not simply books with specific rules and injunctions on manners and deportment but also related works of advice on conduct, character building, beauty, and household management, the size of this literature was still considerable.[16] Some etiquette books were directed to specific audiences—such as children, young men or women, bachelors—but most addressed a general readership. The author of *The American Code of Manners* (1880), a columnist for the popular magazine *The American Queen* in direct contact with a portion of her audience, declared that she wrote her books in response to letters "from young ladies in the West and East; from young housekeepers who are beginning, far from the great cities, the first arduous attempts at dinner-giving; from young men who are rising in the world, and who are beginning to aspire toward that knowledge of society from which they have been debarred by a youth

[14] Timothy Edward Howard, *Excelsior; or, Essays on Politeness, Education, and the Means of Attaining Success in Life* (Baltimore: Kelly and Piet, 1868), 49.

[15] Arthur M. Schlesinger, *Learning How to Behave: A Historical Study of American Etiquette Books* (New York: Macmillan, 1946), 18, 34.

[16] The most complete (but by no means definitive) bibliography of American etiquette books lists 236 separate titles, a number issued in multiple editions, published in the United States before 1900. Some books, however, were published under more than one title, so that the list contains repetitions. See Mary Reed Bobbitt, "A Bibliography of Etiquette Books Published in America Before 1900," *Bulletin of the New York Public Library* 51 (Dec. 1947): 687–720.

of industry; from elderly people, to whom fortune has come late, but whose children begin to wish to know how to take their places in the gay world."[17]

Etiquette manuals were thus part of a larger democratization of gentility in nineteenth-century America. An extensive middle-class market quickly developed for mass-produced imitations of costly luxuries that transformed the appearance and character of the home. Bourgeois Americans avidly purchased balloon-frame houses designed according to widely published architectural plans and furnished them with steel engravings and chromolithographs, an upright piano in the parlor, and a New Haven clock on the mantelpiece.[18] Etiquette writers joined a host of other advisers in teaching those who wished to be thought respectable and successful how to perform various social practices, many of which represented historic innovations in the nineteenth century. These included such newly defined "necessities" as frequent bathing and meticulous grooming,[19] understanding the increasingly specialized furnishings and functions of different rooms in a stylish household, administering servants, conducting oneself properly in the areas of shopping, business, social exchanges, and public deportment in general in the nineteenth-century city.

Nowhere was this transformation more sweeping than in the conduct of dining in the middle-class household. Early in the nineteenth century, pewter, glassware, and china dishes began to supplant wooden trenchers and tankards. With the introduction of machine-made glassware, china, and cutlery, this change accelerated rapidly, so that by 1897 Sears, Roebuck and Company displayed in its catalog page after page of specialized pieces, including a bon-bon serving spoon, "solid silver, with gold plated bowl," for $1.15. At the beginning of the century, most table forks still had two sharp prongs. One held such a fork in the left hand and, after cutting a piece of food, raised it upward with the fork still in the left, then used the flat, rounded blade of the knife in one's right to put the food in one's mouth.[20] But as the two-tined fork yielded to forks

[17] Wesley R. Andrews, *The American Code of Manners* (New York: W. R. Andrews, 1880), i.

[18] On this point see Richard D. Brown, *Modernization: The Transformation of American Life, 1600–1865* (New York: Hill and Wang, 1976), and Nathan Rosenberg, *Technology and Economic Growth* (New York: Harper and Row, 1972).

[19] See Claudia and Richard Bushman, "The Early History of Cleanliness in America," paper presented at Delaware Seminar, University of Delaware, 27 October 1983.

[20] Richard J. Hooker, *Food and Drink in America: A History* (Indianapolis: Bobbs-Merrill, 1981), 97–98.

John F. Kasson

FIG. 4 *Children's birthday party, New York. Courtesy The Byron Collection, Museum of the City of New York.*

[21] However, Esther B. Aresty speculates that Europeans were as right-handed in their use of forks as Americans until around the 1840s, when it began to be fashionable to keep the fork in the left hand. See *The Best Behavior* (New York: Simon and Schuster, 1970), 175.

James Deetz offers still another explanation of the idiosyncratic American use of the fork. He suggests that because forks came into general use much later in colonial New England than in England, even though the colonies imported round-ended knives instead of the pointed blades of old, Americans came to use spoons far more than the English to eat their food. When at last forks were adopted in the eighteenth century, Americans proceeded to employ them like spoons, after they cut their food. See *In Small Things Forgotten: The Archaeology of Early American Life* (Garden City, N.Y.: Anchor Press/ Doubleday, 1977), 123.

[22] Nicholas B. Wainwright, ed., *A Philadelphia Perspective: The Diary of Sidney George Fisher Covering the Years 1834–1871* (Philadelphia: Historical Society of Pennsylvania, 1967), 50.

with three, then four tines, such two-handed eating became a mark of vulgarity. The cumbersome and characteristically American practice developed, whereby one transferred the fork from left to right after cutting a piece of food, and only then raised it to one's mouth.[21]

This procedure was sufficiently established by 1838 for the Philadelphia diarist Sidney Fisher to note his disgust when a man he respected "ate with his knife, smacked his lips, [and] wiped his face & mouth with a red silk handkerchief instead of a napkin."[22]

In 1835, the artist D. C. Johnston drew a cartoon satirizing a farmer's son who had made himself into a dandy, returning home and swooning at the sight of a two-pronged iron fork. The dialogue reads:

[Dandy:] "O! dear remove that horrible vulgar looking

two pronged iron fork from my plate or it will be the death of me."

[Father:] "Well I wonder now if this is really my son Bob that used to eat his pork & beans in the fields with a dung fork across his lap."

[Mother:] "Dear! dear! what a thing it is to travel to foreign parts to get polished!"[23]

But dandies often had the last laugh. Another polished visitor from foreign parts, Charles Dickens marveled during his American tour in 1842 how his fellow passengers on a Pennsylvania canal boat "thrust the broad-bladed knives and the two-pronged forks further down their throats than I ever saw the same weapons go before, except in the hands of a skilled juggler."[24] Opponents of the new fashion might grumble that eating peas with a fork was like "eating soup with a knitting needle," but to no avail.[25] The ascendancy of the fork in the cause of refinement was irresistible. So modish did the fork become that one social wit proclaimed he took everything with it except afternoon tea.[26] By the time Grover Cleveland ran for president in 1884, an editor's gibe that he ate with his knife rankled so deeply that even after his victory Cleveland refused to shake hands with such a gross slanderer.[27] Not "you are *what* you eat," but "you are *how* you eat," became in effect the maxim of the refined.

Such refinement was often painstakingly acquired. Nineteenth-century etiquette writers knew as well as any modern parent how tortuously children mastered the rigors of table etiquette (fig. 4). Where they especially differed from most modern parents was in the depths of their conviction that children retraced the slow, ascending steps of Western civilization as a whole from savagery to refinement. From infancy onward, in the manner in which one ate, one gradually imbibed the lessons of modern civilization—to discipline the cravings of the stomach and the "lower" body by force of intellect, will, and habit. Declared one etiquette manual, "Eating is so entirely

[23] D. C. Johnston, "The Farmers Son Metamorphosed into a finished exquisite," *Scraps,* No. 6 (Boston: D. C. Johnston, 1835), pl. 4, American Antiquarian Society.

[24] Charles Dickens, *American Notes* (1842; reprint, London: Oxford University Press, 1957), 146.

[25] Russell Lynes, *The Domesticated Americans* (New York: Harper and Row, 1963), 182, quoting a source from the 1860s.

[26] Mary Elizabeth Sherwood, *Manners and Social Usages* (New York: Harper and Brothers, 1897), 361.

[27] Schlesinger, *Learning How to Behave,* 41.

FIG. 5 *"The Political Poor Rela-*
tion," reprinted, by permission,
from Roger Butterfield, The American Past *(New York: Simon and*
Schuster, 1947), 258.

FIG. 6 *Joseph Keppler, "The*
Bosses of the Senate," Puck,
23 January 1889.

[28] [Cornelia Holroyd Richards],
At Home and Abroad; or, How to
Behave (New York: Evans and
Brittan, 1853), 26.

[29] The literature of table manners
is in this sense allied in its broader
aims to the literature of sexual
purity aiming to control male
orgasmic excess; see Carroll Smith-
Rosenberg, "Sex as Symbol in
Victorian America," in Salzman,
Prospects 5:51–70.

a sensual, animal gratification, that unless it is conducted with much delicacy, it becomes unpleasant to others."[28] Such a remark helps to illuminate the Victorian prudery that governed dining as well as sexuality. Denying the sexual impulses of the child, authorities nonetheless sought to contain them. The lessons of repression and sublimation, once learned at the table, could be carried to the bedroom and to the world at large.[29]

The bodily symbolism involved in Victorian table manners had broader social dimensions as well. As the anthropologist

FIG. 7 *Luther Daniels Bradley,*
"Design for a Union Station,"
1907. Courtesy The Swann Collec-
tion of Caricature and Cartoon,
Library of Congress.

Mary Douglas has argued, the rituals that different cultures assign to the human body allow it to serve as a symbol for society at large. In the ways people fed their physical bodies, they expressed larger concerns about the needs and perils of the social body as well.[30] The rapid growth of later nineteenth-century America raised disturbing questions about the relationship of society's members. A prominent image of unrestrained greed was of banqueters with bulging stomachs, aghast at the presence of a ragged intruder, with whom they would not think of dining. For example, an 1891 cartoon entitled "The Political Poor Relation" depicted a thin and ragged American farmer supplicating a group of tariff-gorged industrialists. While the farmer's plight goes unattended, congressional waiters including William McKinley offer the party free whiskey and tobacco, and other congressional musicians play the "High Tariff Kinder Sinfonie." Meanwhile, the scent of

[30] See Mary Douglas, *Purity and Danger: An Analysis of the Concept of Pollution and Taboo* (New York: Praeger, 1966), 120–24; *Natural Symbols: Explorations in Cosmology* (New York: Random House, 1973), esp. 12; and Douglas, *Implicit Meanings: Essays in Anthropology* (London: Routledge and Kegan Paul, 1975), "Do Dogs Laugh? A Cross-cultural Approach to Symbolism," 87.

FIG. 8 *Thomas Nast,* Harper's
Weekly, *3 August 1872.*

THEY ARE SWALLOWING EACH OTHER.

a war tariff wafts in from the congressional kitchen (fig. 5).[31]
The cartoonist Joseph Keppler penned a related image in 1889
when he protested the dominance of the U.S. Senate by the
trusts, which he depicted as monstrously bloated moneybags.
A sign on the wall bluntly declared, "This is a Senate of the
Monopolists, by the Monopolists, and for the Monopolists";
the people's entrance is marked "Closed" (fig. 6).

Another image of loss of control was a devouring figure,
swallowing everything in reach. A case in point is the witty
"Design for a Union Station," which lampooned railroad mag-
nate Edward H. Harriman's monopolistic appetites (fig. 7). In
some depictions, such a figure lost all sense of restraint and
turned social cannibal. The fervently Republican cartoonist
Thomas Nast used such an image to devastating effect in 1872
in caricaturing the ability of Liberal Republican Horace
Greeley, Tammany Hall, and Southern Democrats to swallow
each others' positions and unite behind Greeley's candidacy

[31] Roger Butterfield, *The American Past* (New York: Simon and
Schuster, 1947), 258.

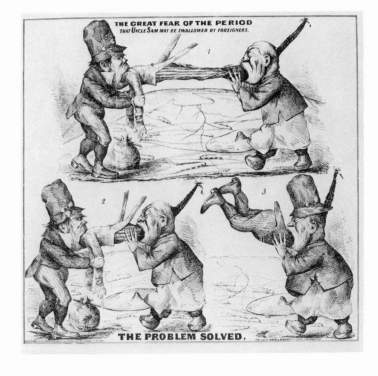

THE GREAT FEAR OF THE PERIOD
THAT UNCLE SAM MAY BE SWALLOWED BY FOREIGNERS.

THE PROBLEM SOLVED.

FIG. 9 *"The Great Fear of the Period." Courtesy Library of Congress.*

(fig. 8). Even more nastily, a contemporary cartoon, "The Great Fear of the Period," expressed nativists' alarm over immigration by sketching an Irishman and a Chinese consuming Uncle Sam simultaneously, with the Chinese swallowing the Irish in the next gulp (fig. 9).

By cultivating practices of refined dining, social conservatives presented an alternative model of social incorporation and growth (fig. 10). According to this model, diners might properly enjoy abundance and, if their means allowed, even luxury, but the appetites were satisfied in a quiet and orderly way, and the cool control of intellect never faltered for an instant. The ritual structure of Victorian table manners mediated between contending needs that were central to the maintenance of social order: between individual appetite and communal order, bodily satisfaction and social modesty, egalitarianism and hierarchy, public and private.

FIG. 10 *"Gentility in the Dining Room," illustration from Thomas E. Hill,* Hill's Manual of Social and Business Forms *(1885; reprint, Chicago: Quadrangle Books, 1971).*

[32] Louise Fiske Bryson, *Every-Day Etiquette: A Manual of Good Manners* (New York: W. D. Kerr, 1890), 97.

[33] It is significant that a key chapter in the modern civil rights movement began when in 1960 four neatly dressed black college students took seats at a "whites only" lunch counter at Woolworth's in Greensboro, North Carolina. See William H. Chafe, *Civilities and Civil Rights: Greensboro, North Carolina, and the Black Struggle for Freedom* (New York: Oxford University Press, 1980).

Because the act of dining carried such high ritual stakes, it needed to be performed in protected circumstances. Etiquette advisers warned against eating in public, whether on the street, in a public place of amusement, or in a railroad coach. Sighed one writer sadly, "The pleasure of travelling is often greatly marred by the needless spectacle of others eating."[32] Among proponents of refinement, to eat or be forced to see another eat promiscuously or immodestly constituted a kind of social obscenity. Just as inviting someone to dine formed a social bond, so eating, if only by necessity, in another's company joined the diners in an ambiguous act of social incorporation. Social conservatives encouraged the increased segmentation of dining practices in the second half of the nineteenth century.[33] They applauded the growing tendency among middle-class Americans to live in private houses or apartments rather than in boarding houses, and, although they encouraged families to invite others to dinner, they extolled such an invitation as "the highest social compliment" and one not to be extended lightly.

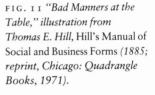

FIG. 11 *"Bad Manners at the Table," illustration from Thomas E. Hill*, Hill's Manual of Social and Business Forms *(1885; reprint, Chicago: Quadrangle Books, 1971).*

Table manners emerged as the supreme test of refinement, character, and (to use the catch-all term so dear to the hearts of nineteenth-century advisers) "good-breeding." In fashionable society, proper deportment at table was the great initiation ritual. The vulgar and inept, the thoughtless and greedy, as well as parvenus and social counterfeits—all risked "instant detection"[34] and exposure in any of the myriad possible violations of proper etiquette in the course of a meal (fig. 11). Even if they avoided an actual misstep, the very pains they would have to devote to their conduct would betray them.

A simple invitation to dinner might thus pose a challenge for the social novice, but not all got off so easy. As families of great wealth sought to consolidate their social positions as an untitled American nobility, they gave dinners of unprecedented elaboration and luxury, at times reaching such heights of excess as the horseback dinner given by C. K. G. Billings in 1903 to celebrate the opening of his new stables (fig. 12). Clearly such entertainments lay beyond the means of all but the

[34] James Dabney McCabe, *The National Encyclopedia of Business and Social Forms* (Philadelphia: National Publishing Co., 1884), 428.

FIG. 12 *Photograph of horseback dinner, Sherry's Restaurant. Courtesy The Byron Collection, Museum of the City of New York.*

wealthiest, but etiquette advisers held their standard up to middle-class readers even as they urged those of modest means to give simpler dinners. That great institution of the late nineteenth century, the formal dinner, loomed before the socially insecure as an excruciating ordeal by fork, "the great trial"[35] on which one's social reputation depended.

What might such a dinner entail? Let us consider what late nineteenth-century etiquette books advised on the subject, beginning with the reception of the invitation.

As a private and honorific request to a private gathering, such an invitation normally came not by post but by a personal messenger. Guests were expected to respond punctually—"a delay is unpardonable"—by messenger in return. Each guest, of course, did not know precisely who would attend, but, in the language of one manual, because at dinner people come into

[35] Ibid.

"closer contact than at a dance, or any other kind of a party," one could be assured that all would be "of the same standing in society" as oneself.[36]

All the rituals comprising the formal dinner demanded attentive and disciplined participation among hosts, guests, and servants. Guests arrived promptly in ceremonial garb, ladies in full dress costumes, gentlemen in evening dress with tails. Advisers castigated those miscreants who were not strictly punctual in their appearance. Arriving early could discommode one's hosts, who might be dressing themselves and making last-minute preparations.[37] In addition, warned one author, "you might excite the suspicion that you came so early to make sure of the feast—a certain sign of greediness."[38] Fifteen minutes was the most a host need allow a tardy guest. Then, in this era before cocktails became part of the dining process, the butler entered the drawing room and quietly announced dinner; or, "better still," he caught the eye of the hostess and bowed. Then, even among supposed social equals, there followed a brief ritual of precedence. The host led the way, escorting the lady most honored on his left. The other gentlemen followed with their assigned dinner partners, with younger members of the dinner party giving way to their elders, and the hostess came last with the gentleman of honor, who sat at her right.[39]

A social novice might then give a sigh of relief and think he could relax and eat, but he would be wrong. It was precisely at the table that the rituals of self-control and polished social performance grew most exacting.

Even so simple an act as seating oneself posed perils. "Be seated with ease," advised one writer, "without rattling your chair; not so far from the table as to endanger your dress in taking food or drink nor so near as to press against the table and shake it at every movement of your body. Unfold your napkin and lay it across your knees, never pinning it over your breast like an alderman [whom the genteel regarded as virtually synonymous with a saloonkeeper] or a slobbering infant."[40]

[36] John C. Young, *Our Deportment*, rev. ed. (Detroit: F. B. Dickerson and Co., 1883), 106. James Bethuel Smiley makes this same point in *Modern Manners and Social Forms* (Chicago: James B. Smiley, 1889), 162.

[37] See [John A. Ruth], *Decorum, a Practical Treatise on Etiquette and Dress of the Best American Society*, rev. by S. L. Louis (New York: Union Publishing House, 1882), 92.

[38] Howard, *Excelsior*, 83.

[39] Smiley, *Modern Manners*, 167–68.

[40] Howard, *Excelsior*, 84.

Once seated, the guest might scan a handwritten menu listing a meal of monumental proportions.[41] Were it served all at once, it might appear as a gross indulgence of appetite. Instead, to give formality, dignity, and order to the occasion, the meal proceeded in a strict and stately progression, with each dish served as a course in itself. These courses mounted in scale and importance from the relatively simple, light, and uncooked to the richer and more lavishly prepared. The elaboration of structure in the meal itself certified the diners' place in the larger social hierarchy.[42]

It began, typically, with raw oysters and champagne. Then waiters offered a choice of a white or brown soup and poured sherry. Then fish with Chablis. Next an entrée, such as asparagus or sweet corn. Then a slice of the roast (with claret and champagne). After that, perhaps some Roman punch (a watery ice made of lemon juice, sugar, beaten egg whites, and rum) to freshen the palate for the courses to follow—game such as canvasback duck (Madeira and port); salad; cheese; pastry or pudding; ices and sweet dishes. *Then* liqueurs. *Then* fruit such as grapes, peaches, or pears, accompanied by sherry or claret. *And then* waiters passed nuts, raisins, sugar plums, and dried ginger.

At the end of the meal, the hostess silently bowed to the lady at the right of the host, and all rose. Gentlemen sometimes remained by themselves at table for a quarter hour with their wine and cigars, liqueurs and cognac. Then they joined the ladies in the drawing room for demitasse, bon-bons and other dainties, and brandy.

Advisers recommended a well-modulated pace. They allowed a maximum of two hours even for a formal dinner, and recommended an hour or ninety minutes.[43] (It is perhaps fair to note parenthetically that the ideal body types of the period were decidedly fuller than in our own time.)

During the entire dinner, whether a simple meal or a stupendous feast like the one described, diners avoided commenting on the food before them, even in praise. Such remarks

[41] This remained true even when, by the turn of the century, etiquette advisers were noting that meals were no longer as large as previously. For example, Ellin Graven Learned, *The Etiquette of New York To-day* (New York: F. A. Stokes, 1906), 85: "Short dinners are the modern fashion. The menu consists, as a general rule, of grapefruit, canapes of caviar, soup, fish, an entree, a roast with two vegetables, game and salad, dessert and fruit." "Cheese," she added in the next breath, "is sometimes served after the game. If artichokes or asparagus are served they are separate courses."

[42] See Mary Douglas, "Deciphering a Meal," in *Myth, Symbol, and Culture*, ed. Clifford Geertz (New York: Norton, 1971), 61–81.

[43] Smiley, *Modern Manners*, 175.

would be too naked an expression of "animal and sensual gratification" over mankind's "intellect . . . and . . . moral nature."[44] According to these rituals, eating was such a private act that it was possible only if one pretended to ignore it.

Thus, diners sought to cloak their bodily needs and invest the occasion with dignity by distancing themselves from organic processes. Symbolic demonstrations of bodily control testified to their commitment to social order and constraint.[45]

Such controls took a number of ritual expressions. First, diners minimized their own appetites and sought to avoid any hint of greediness. Etiquette authorities warned them not to eat hastily, or to take large mouthfuls, tilt a soup plate for the last spoonful, "scrape the last morsel of food from your place," or attempt to drain the last drop from a glass.[46]

Polite dining also meant that one's food was touched as little as possible. No matter how much handling might be involved in the meal's preparation, in the dining room servants and guests participated in elaborate rituals of purity. Although neither group wore gloves (men and women alike removed theirs as they sat down), each waiter wrapped a napkin around his thumb in serving so that his hand never touched the surface of plates or dishes. Some advisers applauded the custom of having servants pass dishes to and from guests on little silver or brass trays instead of with their hands.[47] To minimize the carving of meat in the presence of guests, the passing of dishes at table, and the sight of leftovers shared in common, dining *à la Russe* became the fashion: all the plates were prepared elsewhere and served individually.

A hierarchy of cutlery itself had developed, and etiquette advisers reminded their readers not only to keep their knife blades out of their mouths but also to minimize the knife's use in general. One should use the fork, the utensil of greatest refinement, whenever possible, and resort to one's fingers only in a very few cases. In eating fruit, for example, one book noted: "It is always better to use a fork, even at the peril of seeming affected than to offend the taste of another by making

[44] Howard, *Excelsior,* 87.
[45] This is what Mary Douglas has called the "purity rule." See *Natural Symbols,* 12, 16; see also Douglas, *Purity and Danger.*
[46] Smiley, *Modern Manners,* 183.
[47] Ibid., 174.

a mess with the fingers, as some careless people often do."[48] The sight of teeth marks on a partially eaten piece of bread, fruit, or an ear of corn filled etiquette authorities with special disgust. Such an unmistakable imprint of bodily processes undercut all the elaborate rituals designed to keep them at a distance.

An equally offensive and naked act of ingestion was eating or drinking noisily. Such a lapse was taken to betray an almost hopelessly coarse and inconsiderate nature. For such offenders, the "laws" of etiquette were necessary to provide the social discipline that the "well-bred" possessed instinctively. With withering contempt, one writer denounced these boors:

> No sensitive person can hear any one taking his soup, coffee, or other liquid, without positive annoyance. Yet, those who would be very unwilling to consider themselves ill-bred are constantly guilty of such breach of politeness. The defect is that they are not so sensitive as those with whom they come in contact. They would not be disturbed by the offense; they never imagine, therefore, that any one else can be. It is for them that rules of etiquette are particularly designed. Were their instinct correct, they would not need the rule, which, from the absence of instinct, appears to them irrational, purely arbitrary.[49]

All the little gestures of bodily adjustment and self-engrossment that were to be avoided in polite society demanded especially precise regulation at the table. Diners were admonished not to scratch their heads, to pick their teeth, or to make similar gestures, and indeed they were advised sternly to "keep the hands below the table when unoccupied."[50]

Refined diners sought particularly to stifle all activities that might draw attention to the internal workings of the body, such as coughing, sneezing, and nose blowing. "Never if possible, cough or sneeze at the table," one writer declared. "If you feel the paroxysm coming on, leave the room."[51]

More generally, diners were expected to demonstrate their

[48] Ibid., 188–89.
[49] "Table Customs," *Scribner's Monthly* 8 (1874): 627.
[50] Smiley, *Modern Manners,* 186.
[51] Ruth, *Decorum,* 213. See also Smiley, *Modern Manners,* 185; on nose wiping, see 184.

own refinement, self-control, and subordination to the social gathering by guarding against disruptions of all sorts. They regulated emotional displays as rigorously as they did their bodies, avoiding both extremes of sadness and boisterous laughter. As one adviser declared, "Moods should be our own secrets."[52] Diners were encouraged not simply to fall silent but to engage in conversation while eating, keeping the table talk light and steering away from "heated discussions" and "heavy or abstruse topics."[53]

Here is a model conversation between two guests, as supplied by one authority on manners:

> Having seated themselves, and exchanged a few comments (of course flattering), on the table decorations, the lady, wishing to ascertain whether her companion was one of the silent diners-out, might say:
>
> "Some people do not care to eat and talk at the same time, but prefer to let what few comments they make come in between the courses."
>
> [HE:] "A man must be a dull fellow who cannot do both, with satisfaction to his neighbor if not to himself."
>
> [SHE:] "Then I may talk to you without fear of interrupting your enjoyment of your dinner? But you speak as though it were easier to please your neighbor than yourself."
>
> [HE:] "Set down that speech to my gallantry. Ladies are so good natured that they take the will for the deed, while my modesty precludes my taking credit for any efforts of mine."[54]

The prospect of such repartee perhaps also consoled the uninvited.

If despite all one's efforts at grace and refinement, an accident occurred—a spilled wineglass, an upset plate—what then? "Do not appear disconcerted, nor apologize while at the table," etiquette authorities advised. Calmness and self-composure should reign above all.[55] Part of the hostess's duty

[52] [Abby Buchanan Longstreet], *Social Etiquette of New York* (New York: D. Appleton and Co., 1879), 129.

[53] Smiley, *Modern Manners*, 185.

[54] Mary Simmerson (Cunningham) Logan and others, *The Home Manual* (Chicago: H. J. Smith and Co., 1889), 47–48.

[55] Smiley, *Modern Manners*, 182.

in such minor emergencies was to aid the hapless guest by standing as "a model of serenity, tact, and self-possession. . . . If her precious china and her rare glass are broken before her eyes, she must seem to take but little or no notice of it."[56]

Once the meal had concluded, guests were expected to remain and talk for an hour or so. Leaving too soon might suggest that one came merely for the food and not the company.[57] Similarly, when the time came to depart, profuse expressions of gratitude were frowned upon. As one adviser wrote, "guests may express the pleasure the occasion has afforded them, but further thanks are now considered old fashioned."[58] Recipients of invitations, whether they actually attended the dinner or not, were also expected to make a brief formal call upon the host within ten days after the occasion. And ultimately, of course, they were obliged to repay the "debt" of hospitality.

What may we conclude from such dining rituals? The life of all communities is dialectical in nature, and no ritual may be said to epitomize wholly a society's concerns. Nonetheless, social rituals have an importance far beyond what we ordinarily acknowledge. The ceremonial forms that govern a given occasion shape its content and possibilities in profound ways, whether its participants are aware of it or not. They are not simply a neutral medium of communication—nothing is. They provide devices that frame, channel, and control experience, admitting certain possibilities, foreclosing others.[59]

The rituals of polite Victorian dining sought to elevate and protect the individual dignity and self-possession of all participants. They demanded and sought to develop, above all, the virtues of mutual respect, tact, and self-possession. Adopting and further refining the ceremonial forms of the nobility, advocates of polite dining insisted upon their special relevance in a democracy. Here, if individuals were to be masterless, it was all the more essential that they be masters of themselves. In Victorian table manners and especially in the conduct of the formal dinner, one may see a great effort to maintain social

[56] Young, *Our Deportment,* 118.

[57] Howard, *Excelsior,* 89: "After enjoying the hospitality of another's board, it is not in good taste to depart immediately, as though you were indeed a boarder. . . ."

[58] Smiley, *Modern Manners,* 177.

[59] Douglas, *Purity and Danger,* 62–63.

order, hierarchy, and individuation through the very ritual structure of dining.

As we have seen, an important element in these table manners was a recognition that the process of eating might reduce all involved to an animal level of appetite and competition, a Hobbesian "war of all against all." In a period of American history when economic competition was at its fiercest, rituals of refined dining guarded against the spread of such struggles into the private realm of friendship and family. Nature, and even business, might be "red in tooth and claw," but the domestic circle could provide a refuge of sympathy, harmony, and refinement.

This tightening of controls also guarded, less clearly but equally effectively, against a stripping away of social distinctions and the achievement of a celebratory human bondedness, what the anthropologist Victor Turner has called "communitas."[60] In all societies, as Turner has observed, "a contrast is posited between the notion of society as a differentiated, segmented system of structured positions . . . and society as a homogeneous, undifferentiated *whole*."[61] Segmentation had become one of the great principles of refinement as well as an increasingly important aspect of American society as a whole. Advocates of civility and refinement may well have sensed that the act of sharing a meal might subvert that segmentation, not in favor of barbarism but of some new radical sort of leveling. Potentially, dining might usher in a new kind of fellowship, a melting of individual reserve and a breakdown of social norms into a changed collectivity.

Such a fellowship might take many forms—but to indicate how such possibilities were held in check, let me touch briefly on the dining ritual of fellowship and transformation most familiar to late nineteenth-century Americans: the Last Supper. Etiquette advisers never tired of insisting that the basis of all politeness was the Golden Rule, and that the epitome of the gentleman was Jesus. But a Last Supper conducted according

[60] Victor Turner, *The Ritual Process: Structure and Anti-Structure* (Ithaca: Cornell University Press, 1969), esp. 131.

[61] Victor Turner, *Dramas, Fields, and Metaphors: Symbolic Action in Human Society* (Ithaca: Cornell University Press, 1974), 237.

to the etiquette of a late nineteenth-century dinner party would have been impossible. The rituals of polite dining simply would not have permitted it. Such a departure would have threatened to forge participants into a new kind of communion that would subvert the established order.[62] My point in making such a comparison between Victorian dining and the Last Supper is neither to accuse advocates of refined dining of hypocrisy nor to make light of the Gospels. It is rather to offer one final illustration of the larger stakes that rituals of dining may contain in their conduct and their symbolism, and more specifically, to underscore the profound conservatism implicit in late nineteenth-century table manners.

A genteel Victorian Last Supper would have been impossible, first, because it is ludicrous to imagine Jesus and his apostles donning formal dress and participating in the ceremonies of private ownership and display. Their radical insistence upon poverty and acceptance of the lowly would have subverted the genteel concern with the maintenance of status and the enshrinement of private goods.

In addition, the Victorian emphasis upon prescribed social forms and procedures would have amounted to pharisaism, a strict insistence upon the letter of social ritual in such a way as to kill the spirit. One imagines etiquette advisers objecting that Jesus couldn't possibly invite *twelve* people for dinner, since then there would be thirteen at the table—a number always to be avoided because someone might consider it unlucky. Jesus would simply have to include another guest or else trim his invitations. Similarly, Jesus' warning that one would betray him would have violated the host's pose of bland good humor. Instead of introducing profound and abstruse matters, advisers might object, he above all should steer conversation toward light chit-chat.

More fundamentally, Jesus' insistence that the shared bread and wine be regarded as his body and blood in holy communion would have struck Victorians as a revolting analogy.

[62] The Last Supper, of course, was also horrifying in the context of Jewish dietary laws of its own day. See the illuminating discussion in Gillian Feeley-Harnik, *The Lord's Table: Eucharist and Passover in Early Christianity* (Philadelphia: University of Pennsylvania Press, 1981).

They located threats to purity without, in the objects one ate and the way one ate them. He insisted that the great threats to purity lay within.[63] He offered salvation through Grace; they sought distinction through the social graces.

Finally, Jesus' washing of the disciples' feet after supper would have thrown etiquette advisers into consternation. In Victorian dining practices, each individual tended to his own ritual cleansing, and any suggestion that it required another would have been an affront. In addition, Jesus' act would have seemed both unseemly bodily contact and a shocking loss of dignity on the part of the host in stooping to the task of a servant.

In short, Victorian table manners were designed to set careful limits upon the possibilities of social interaction and communion, to reinforce and justify existing social relationships rather than to change them. They checked any sort of deviation from the paths of social propriety, whether they led in the direction of individual assertion or communal transformation.

[63] See John Murray Cuddihy, *The Ordeal of Civility* (New York: Basic Books, 1974), 158.

The Vision of the Dining Room

PLAN BOOK DREAMS AND MIDDLE-CLASS

REALITIES

CLIFFORD E. CLARK, JR.

N the middle decades of the nineteenth century, architects, writers, family reformers, and housing developers published thousands of plan books with advice on how to design a more up-to-date house. Although this promotional literature glorified an ideal toward which people were to strive rather than documented actual houses that were built, it provides a valuable and hitherto unused source for understanding the changes taking place in middle-class dining rooms in the post–Civil War period. A careful examination of the most popular plan books reveals that the dining room in the second half of the century took on a new importance as the hallmark of the achievement of middle-class respectability. Even an occasional critic such as the architect Sereno Todd tacitly admitted the new importance that middle-class women attached to the design and decoration of their dining rooms. Writing in his 1870 plan book, *Todd's*

FIG. 1 *This idealized vision of the middle-class family appeared as the frontispiece for the 1869 edition of one of the best-selling advice books at mid-century, Catharine Beecher and Harriet Beecher Stowe's* American Woman's Home *(New York: J. B. Ford and Co., 1869).*

Country Homes and How to Save Money, Todd complained that "a frugal meal tastes better in the kitchen, than in an uncheerful dining-room."

> Most people feel more in an element that is congenial to a good nature, when they are in the kitchen, than when encircled by the restraints and constraints of a parlor, that the fastidious housewife deems too nice to be occupied. ... The rule is, the country through—at least so far as my observations have extended—that most farmers erect a nice and expensive house, with a costly parlor or two, and furnished with beautiful carpets, window-shades and other adjuncts of a parlor, and go and look into the-almost-sacred apartment about once a week; and in many instances, the parlor is carpeted; the dining-room is a sacred sanctorum; the kitchen is too nice for occupancy and the family live in the wood-house, or in some scavenger's shanty, that has been joined on the farther end of all the buildings.[1] (Fig. 1)

Todd's complaint that special decorations and rules about table manners had made the dining room inhospitable was clearly an exception to the growing chorus of approval in post–Civil War America for giving the dining room an enlarged role in middle-class family life. What provoked this refrain? What can we learn from it about changes in the design and decoration of the middle-class dining room? An answer to these questions, I suggest, can be found by comparing the information in plan books about the changing nature of middle-class houses with surviving evidence about individual families. Because the dining room was a particular space within the house whose design and use changed in the late nineteenth century, hints about its design and decoration can be inferred by looking at the common features shared by most plan book models. Although not literal blueprints for actual behavior, plan books, I would argue, are useful for providing evidence both about the changing use of space within the house and

[1] Sereno E. Todd, *Todd's Country Homes and How to Save Money* (Hartford: Hartford Publishing Co., 1870), 55–56.

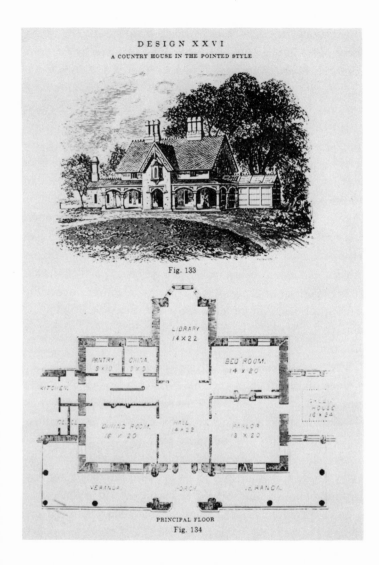

DESIGN XXVI

A COUNTRY HOUSE IN THE POINTED STYLE

Fig. 133

LIBRARY
14 × 22

PANTRY
8 × 10

CHINA
8 × 3

BED ROOM.
14 × 20

KITCHEN.

DINING ROOM.
16 × 20

HALL
14 × 28

PARLOR
18 × 20

VERANDA

PORCH

VERANDA

PRINCIPAL FLOOR
Fig. 134

FIG. 2 *Andrew Jackson
Downing's plan book* The Architecture of Country Houses *(New
York: D. Appleton and Co., 1850)
supplied complete plans together
with a new aesthetic rationale for
house design. Houses were supposed to be a reflection of the
individuality of their owners.*

about the place of the dining room in the cult of middle-class
respectability.

Any analysis of plan book dining rooms should begin with
the recognition that a major transformation took place at mid-
century within the plan book publishing industry itself. The
earliest "builder's guides," such as Asher Benjamin's *American
Builder's Companion* (1806), had primarily provided detailed .

Clifford E. Clark, Jr.

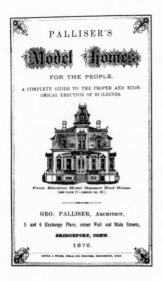

PALLISER'S

Model Homes

FOR THE PEOPLE.

A COMPLETE GUIDE TO THE PROPER AND ECON-
OMICAL ERECTION OF BUILDINGS.

Front Elevation Model Mansart Roof House.
(SEE PAGE 17—DESIGN NO. 58.)

GEO. PALLISER, ARCHITECT,

5 and 6 Exchange Place, corner Wall and Main Streets,

BRIDGEPORT, CONN.

1876.

GOULD & STILES, STEAM JOB PRINTERS, BRIDGEPORT, CONN.

FIG. 3 *George Palliser's* Model
Homes *(Bridgeport, Conn., 1876)*
was subsidized by advertisements
and sold for only twenty-five cents.
Courtesy American Life Founda-
tion, Watkins Glen, N.Y.

2 Clifford E. Clark, Jr.,
"Domestic Architecture as an Index
to Social History: The Romantic
Revival and the Cult of Domesticity
in America, 1840–1870," *Journal
of Interdisciplinary History* 7, no. 1
(Summer 1976): 33–56; Dell
Upton, "Pattern Books and Profes-
sionalism," *Winterthur Portfolio*
19, nos. 2/3 (Summer/Autumn
1984): 108.

3 James L. Garvin, "Mail-Order
House Plans and American Victorian Architecture," *Winterthur
Portfolio* 16, no. 4 (Winter 1981):
321.

illustrations for doors, windows, and moldings. By the 1850s, these older builder's guides were being replaced by far more comprehensive "plan books" such as Andrew Jackson Downing's *Architecture of Country Houses* (1850), which provided not only full-scale drawings of houses, but also advice about historical styles and proper interior decoration (fig. 2). Beginning slowly between 1800 and 1840, twenty editions of different plan books were published. In the 1850s, this number was increased by ninety-three new books. In the 1870s, an additional fifty-eight new editions of books by authors such as George E. Woodward, Henry Hudson Holly, and Robert W. Shoppell came out; what was even more important, their prices dropped from two or three dollars a book to seventy-five cents or less.[2] Architects began to sell their designs by mail. By 1887, George Palliser of Bridgeport, Connecticut, who ran one of the most successful mail-order house plan businesses, could boast that he had sold more than 75,000 copies of his plans for houses ranging in price from $900 to $7,500 (fig. 3).[3]

The vast expansion of advice and plan books during the nineteenth century was part of a massive campaign to create a new image of the middle-class house. Housing, of course, had always had status implications. Even in the eighteenth century, one could identify the wealthier members of society by the houses they built. Nevertheless, before 1800 there was relatively little explicit justification offered for building a particular kind of house. But from the 1840s on, a flood of plan books began to promote an idea of home that is laden with social and behavioral meaning. In his book *The Model Architect* (1852), Samuel Sloan articulated the popular view of the house as a sacred refuge for the middle-class family when he argued that "no one can measure how much the charms of the home are heightened by adding all the delights of tasteful elegance to the associations which throng its sacred precincts. . . . Indeed, all that is pure in human nature, all the tender affections and gentle endearments of childhood, all the soothing comforts of old age, all that makes memory a blessing, the present delightful, and gives to hope its spur, cluster around that holy place—home."[4] This idealization of the home as the sacred center of middle-class family life, and the emphasis placed on "the delights of tasteful elegance," were to have significant implications for the importance that the middle class attached to the use of the dining room (fig. 4).

Plan books such as Sloan's reveal a conspicuous fact: ownership of a house with a separate dining room had become one of the prime symbols of the achievement of middle-class status. In his popular book *The Architecture of Country Houses*, Andrew Jackson Downing established a pattern of associating different kinds of houses with different income levels that would continue for the rest of the century. Downing divided houses into three categories according to their owners' income—"cottages," designed for those of moderate income, especially "industrious and intelligent mechanics and working men"; "farm-houses," built for those who worked the land and had "no money to spare for ornamental decoration"; and "villas," "the country house of a person of competence or wealth sufficient to build and maintain it with some taste and elegance." Unlike the cottage or the farmhouse, the villa embodied the two traits that were necessary for the achievement of middle- and upper-class status: money and taste. Money without taste was not enough to lift a person to the upper classes.

One important indicator that a family possessed taste was the inclusion in its house of a well-furnished and well-decorated dining room. It is significant, therefore, that when Downing presented plans for working-class cottages in the 1850s, dining rooms were consistently absent (figs. 5 and 6). In place of one, the inexpensive houses had a "living room" or even a "parlor," a flexible space that could be used for multiple purposes. Even large farmhouses, built for men of substantial means, lacked dining rooms (figs. 7 and 8). Perhaps the major reason for the absence of the dining room in such houses, as Sereno Todd later asserted, was that most farm families pre-

The Vision of the Dining Room

FIG. 4 *The importance of the house as a protected retreat for women and personal family relations can be seen in this November 1878 cover for* The Mother's Magazine. *Courtesy Collection of Business Americana, The Smithsonian Institution.*

[4] Samuel Sloan, *The Model Architect* (Philadelphia: E. G. Jones and Co., 1852), 10.

FIGS. 5 and 6 *Andrew Jackson Downing's designs for a "Small Bracketed Cottage" and a "Bracketed Cottage, with Veranda," published in his* Architecture of Country Houses, *show workingmen's houses with no provision for a dining room.*

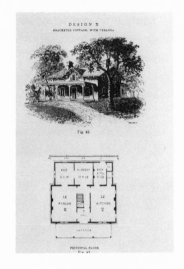

FIGS. 7 and 8 *The large farmhouses depicted in Downing's* Architecture of Country Houses *do not include dining rooms, even though these dwellings were clearly the homes of wealthy families.*

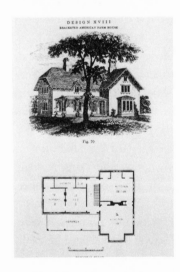

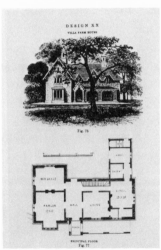

5 Andrew Jackson Downing, *The Architecture of Country Houses* (New York: D. Appleton and Co., 1850), 40, 135, 257.

ferred to eat in the kitchen in order not to risk soiling the rest of the house. Nevertheless, the possession of a well-furnished dining room indicated that the owner of a house had the wealth, the time, and the social knowledge to devote special effort to meal preparation and consumption.[5]

In Downing's most elaborate residences, the dining room was sometimes called a "dining hall," a term that harked back to previous centuries when a major room used for meals and social gatherings was called "the hall" (figs. 9 and 10a and b). Among some plan book writers, an interest persisted in maintaining this more antiquarian view of the room. Although most mid-century plan books did not devote much attention to the dining room, George E. Woodward republished, in his 1867 plan book, *Woodward's Architecture and Rural Art,* an unusually detailed account by a Dr. D. D. Slade describing Slade's ideal vision of the old large, rectangular dining hall in a turn-of-the-century house:

And what would induce us to part with the cheery and happy spirit which this old fire-place continually infuses into our little family—whether at the morning hour, when we first assemble around the table, or at the "children's hour," between daylight and dark, when we gather around its hearth to listen to some oft-read story or to recite some well-known adventure! A Turkey carpet of pleasing colors and thick texture, an article which, in our minds, is always associated with substantial old-fashioned families, contributes greatly to our comfort. An antique side-board, convenient both in its external and internal arrangements, with a half dozen high-backed mahogany chairs, telling of Dutchland, not to forget a more luxurious arm-chair, constitute the movable furniture. Simple, unostentatious woolen curtains hang at the bay and other windows, supported upon black walnut fixtures . . . numerous engravings adorn the wall, not in gilded frames but in those made of hard wood. . . . Beside these ancient clock and bronze candlesticks, numerous little objects, tokens of kind remembrance, adorn the broad and ample mantle-shelf.[6]

Clearly the central feature of this idealized description of an eighteenth-century dining room was its ability to evoke a sense of family cohesiveness. A good dining room, according to the plan books, should reinforce the spiritual unity of the family. In

[6] George E. Woodward, *Woodward's Architecture and Rural Art* (New York: George E. Woodward and Co., 1867), 1:127–29.

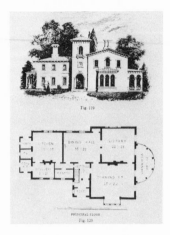

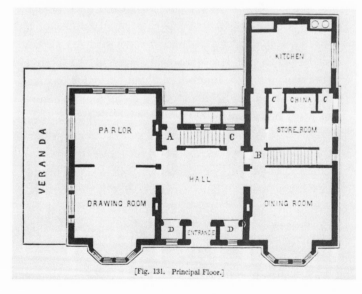

FIGS. 9 and **10a** and **b** *The "dining halls" in these expensive houses from Downing's* Architecture of Country Houses *were a throwback to seventeenth- and eighteenth-century dining arrangements.*

FIG. 11 *This vision of the "Christian Home" from Beecher and Stowe's* American Woman's Home *is the classic image of the middle-class family home as a sheltered retreat, nestled in the world of nature, and therefore implicitly sheltered from the evils associated with urban life.*

that sense, the dining room was to be part of the ideal Christian family home that was promoted by Catharine Beecher and other domestic reformers, a sacred space where the family could commune together. Clearly it fit with the popularity of the Gothic Revival house, the ideal Christian environment that came complete with stained-glass windows, a pump organ, and crosses at the gables (fig. 11).

Implicit in Woodward's citation of Dr. Slade's vision of an eighteenth-century dining room with its large tiled fireplace and low ceiling was the view that although times had changed, a good modern dining room in 1867 should have those features of the older space which would reinforce a sense of family

Clifford E. Clark, Jr.

FIG. 12a and b *Inexpensive houses in the 1880s were still designed without separate dining rooms, as in this example from S. B. Reed's* House-Plans for Everybody *(New York: Orange Judd Co., 1878). Courtesy Avery Architectural and Fine Arts Library, Columbia University.*

Fig. 14.—FRONT ELEVATION.—Scale, 8 feet to 1 inch.

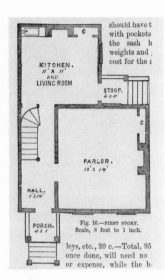

Fig. 16.—FIRST STORY. Scale, 8 feet to 1 inch.

solidarity. Although the modern dining room would not have the Turkey carpet (oriental rug), ancient side-board, etchings in polished hardwood frames, ancient clock, and bronze candlesticks, it should still be a reasonably large, rectangular room, twelve by fourteen or fifteen by eighteen feet. It should have a bay window on the southeast side to let in the morning and evening sun, a convenient pantry and closet, a carpet in some warm, neutral tint, curtains (which were the sign of "good sense and a refined taste"), and plants and flowers whose "silent influence makes all the household more cheerful and better." Finally, Dr. Slade insisted, the decorative scheme of the dining room should fit with the rest of the house.

By the 1870s, therefore, plan book writers had followed the lead of Andrew Jackson Downing, George Woodward, and others, and suggested a generally accepted set of conventions for the placement and decoration of dining rooms. As a perusal of S. B. Reed's *House-Plans for Everybody* (1878) or Daniel T. Atwood's *Country and Suburban Houses* (1871) indicates, well-furnished dining rooms were still an indication of middle-class status: "cheap" (a term used in the plan books), inexpensive laborers' or mechanics' houses still did not contain dining

DESIGN No. 2.

First-floor Plan.

1. Vestibule; 2. Parlor, 15 × 23; 3. Dining-hall, 14 × 18; 4. Dining-room closet; 5. Butler's pantry; 6. Kitchen, 14 × 16; 7. Main stairs; 8. Back stairs; 9. Kitchen closet; 10, 10, 10. Verandas.—*Estimated cost, $4500.*

This is a design for a small cottage of moderate cost. It was intended for an alteration of an ordinary square house, with a kitchen wing, the lines of the house and roof remaining the same, the interior materially changed.

The principal features added are the two bay-windows in front, the one on the right for the parlor, and that on the left accommodating the main staircase, each running the entire height of the building. The space between these windows is used as a hooded porch, with a recessed balcony

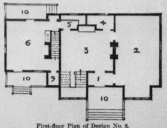

First-floor Plan of Design No. 2.

above, giving the whole a varied and somewhat original aspect. For motives of economy, the main staircase is placed in the dining-hall, the vestibule acting as an entrance to the dining-hall and parlor, so that guests may be introduced into the latter without disturbing the family while at meals.

FIG. 13a and b *One of the new features stressed by Henry Hudson Holly in his plan book* Modern Dwellings *(New York: Harper and Brothers, 1878) was the butler's pantry (the room numbered five on the floor plan) that allowed easy passage to the dining room but also shielded the family and guests from a view of the kitchen.*

rooms (fig. 12a and b). In more expensive house plans, not only were dining rooms featured, but a connecting "butler's pantry," complete with sink and china closet, was also apt to be included.

As architect Henry Hudson Holly, who was obviously hoping to attract wealthy clients, wrote in his plan book *Holly's*

Country Seats (1863), "The ordinary objection to using a dining room for the purposes of family gatherings, is that it must necessarily be occupied by the servants after meals, for removing the service and 'tidying up' generally. Much of this, however, may be obviated by the provision of a butler's pantry, and thus the dining room and hall may be used as sitting rooms, while the library remains for literary purposes." Holly also suggested that architects accommodate the increasing use of sideboards by making sure that if the only wall long enough to contain the sideboard had windows, the windows be elevated and constructed in a horizontal position so that the sideboard could be placed under them (fig. 13a and b).[7]

As Holly's comments suggested, the middle-class dining room in the pre–1880s plan books was intended to be used largely for the family rather than for entertaining guests. Indeed, there was a strong reaction against other attempts that, as one commentator in *Putnam's Magazine* put it, "seek to induce a fashion which has no root in our instincts and relations." The growing interest in room decoration and display promoted by furniture makers and dry goods stores was at first resisted; family reformers insisted that the home should serve the needs of the family rather than function as an instrument of display. A writer in the *Atlantic Monthly* put it even more succinctly when he suggested, "Henceforth he [the guest] is welcome, but he is secondary; it was not for him that the house was built; and if it comes to choosing, he can be dispensed with." This view was in keeping with the mid-century image of the middle-class house as a protected and nurturing refuge from the evils of urban life. The home should be a place where, as Sereno Todd insisted, the Christian family could "worship God, with none to molest or make us afraid." Plan books before the 1880s, therefore, spent relatively little time describing the decoration of the dining room and instead concentrated on detailing the furnishings of the space in the hall and the parlor. As Holly admitted in one of his designs, "This happens

[7] Henry Hudson Holly, *Holly's Country Seats* (New York: D. Appleton and Co., 1863), 75.

to be the dining room, which is seldom occupied for any other than its legitimate purpose; therefore, exterior views are of comparatively small consideration."[8] This is not to say that middle-class families did not occasionally have guests at their meals, but rather that the dining room was intended primarily for family use.

Upper-class families, in contrast, had long made an elaborate ritual of dinner parties. Advice books such as Florence Hartley's *Ladies' Book of Etiquette and Manual of Politeness*, published in 1860, had complete sections on dinner parties and manners. Typical was Hartley's suggestion that "one cook cannot prepare dinner properly for more than ten persons, and three waiters will find ample employment in waiting upon the same number." Hartley recommended that dinner parties for the wealthy be lavish affairs, complete with snowy damask tablecloths, silver or china centerpieces, pyramids of flowers, elaborate silverware, four wineglasses of various sizes per person, and glasses of celery, transparent jellies, and "exquisite little glass plates of pickles." The meal, she added, should begin with soup, which would be followed by a fish course, then oysters, minced veal or lobster, next a roast and vegetables, next pastry and puddings, salad and cheese, and, finally, dessert.[9]

By the 1880s, evidence from the plan books indicates that the more elaborate mealtime rituals formerly limited to the wealthy had started to become more typical, on a smaller scale, in middle-class houses. At the same time, architects and plan book writers were becoming more concerned about the burdens placed upon middle-class women by the need to supervise and prepare these elaborate meals. These two changes—an emphasis on more elaborate meals in a more elaborate setting, and the need for efficiency and labor-saving devices to help women (in part because of the increasing difficulty in finding servants)—were part of a larger movement in the 1880s to improve the status of middle-class women who worked at

[8] "House Building in America," *Putnam's Magazine* 15 (July 1857): 109; "House Building," *Atlantic Monthly* 10 (Oct. 1862): 423; Todd, *Todd's Country Homes*, 33; Holly, *Holly's Country Seats*, 91.

[9] Florence Hartley, *The Ladies' Book of Etiquette and Manual of Politeness* (Boston: G. W. Cottrell, 1860), 88–91.

home, a movement that was to change dramatically the artistic and social standards of middle-class homes toward the end of the century.

During the last third of the nineteenth century, the tremendous expansion of the American economy opened up new opportunities for the middle class and helped change the popular middle-class image of family life from one that stressed the importance of the household as a protected retreat from urban dangers to one that promoted the family as a vehicle for enhancing self-development and creative expression. This view was in part an extension of an older ideal—that the family was the best school for the development of character—and in part the result of a new fascination with the artistic or otherwise creative potential of individual family members. As M. G. Van Rensselaer expressed it in "The Development of American Homes" in *Forum* magazine, "We are learning that the essence of all beauty is *design,* that a clear, coherent idea should underlie every effort, that to get a beautiful house we must build it beautifully and furnish it in a harmonious way."[10]

Although many of the new immigrants who entered the country in this period were penniless, and although almost half of all American families were propertyless, the substantial increases in manufacturing, transportation, and merchandising businesses meant that significantly more people entered the white-collar classes. For these middle-class Americans, salaries replaced wages, and their lives reflected a new sense of abundance and security.

As a consequence, the middle-class suburban home, portrayed in the latest Queen Anne, Eastlake, or French Second Empire styles, was now designed with an emphasis on comfort and consumption that extended into the dining room. Middle-class women at mid-century had been taught from an early age to draw, play the piano, crochet, and design elaborate "female elegancies" that could be displayed around the house. Earlier in the century, many women had, of course, woven cloth and sewn clothes for their families. Spared these chores because of

[10] M. G. Van Rensselaer, "The Development of American Homes," *Forum* 12 (January 1892): 672. See also Robert Grant, "The Art of Living, Home Furnishing, and the Commisariat," *Scribner's* 17 (March 1895): 307–8. For a discussion of the changing popular image of the middle-class family at mid-century, see Clifford E. Clark, Jr., *The American Family Home* (Chapel Hill: University of North Carolina Press, 1986), chaps. 2 and 3.

ready-made shirts and dresses that were available after the Civil War, they now turned their attention to more decorative creations. The new interest in artistic creativity found expression in a wide range of everyday affairs from the decoration of rooms to the preparation of food.

The emphasis on women's artistic potential served as a significant antidote to the failure of the public at large to acknowledge the importance of cleaning, cooking, and housework. In a society where individual identity was increasingly being tied to occupation, where men were thought of in terms of the work they did—be it in law, carpentry, sales, or medicine—women were caught between two attitudes. On the one hand, the middle-class image stressed the gentility of being a "housewife," a term that originated in the Middle Ages but that took on new meaning in the late nineteenth century. On the other, women desired to be given more credit for the work that they actually did at home. Thus many women deliberately cultivated the image of being an artist to increase the public stature of their position in the house.

It was only a short step, then, for plan book authors and family reformers to begin to argue that the house was to be a personal artistic statement—a symbolic representation of what the owner and his wife stood for and valued. The ideal middle-class home thereby became an instrument for creative display. As designer John Brett wrote in the *American Architect and Building News* in 1893, "Civilized man has a want which a tent cannot supply, viz., a place for the exhibition of his treasure, especially the treasure of beauty, for which stability, permanence, and good day-light are wanted. He also requires a base of operations for his enterprises, a museum for his archives and trophies, and above all, for the convenient arrangement of his intellectual resources—for his books and his pictures. He may also require means for the entertainment of his neighbors and his children, and for seeing them to the best advantage."[11]

Decorating the middle-class house thus became a major task

[11] John Brett, "Daylight in the Dwelling House," *American Architect and Building News* 39 (Jan. 1893): 21.

for the housewife. The plan books emphasized the importance of the woman's commitment to fostering beauty. "There is un-limited scope for the exercise of womanly tact and taste in the arrangement and furnishing of every room," suggested archi-tect Frank L. Smith. "What we need in house decoration is, first of all, fitness, and then beauty. But beauty is composed of many elements, —strength, dignity, meaning, character, as well as grace of form and harmony of color. Prettiness is something considerably less than beauty."[12] According to such experts, the extra time spent in decorating the middle-class house was well worth it, because artistic achievement was a sign of a more sophisticated and civilized outlook.

By the 1880s, therefore, the ideal of the artistic middle-class house had become extremely popular. These houses were de-signed to be read like a book whose symbolic meanings would be almost self-evident to contemporaries. The guidebooks and, later, the furniture manufacturers, suggested that the ideal dining room in these houses be organized around some central theme for which the symbolic associations could be gradually perceived (fig. 14). Like a good mystery story, the meaning of the room would unfold gradually. The visitor was a detective, and part of the enjoyment of going to dinner at someone's house came from trying to understand the symbolic meanings of the furnishings. Robert W. Shoppell, author of the popular 1883 plan book *How to Build, Furnish, and Decorate*, made these assumptions explicit in his description of a dining room:

> We sum up the hints on the furnishing of a dining-room by a short description of a room we have in our mind. The walls . . . , are papered with an olive-toned paper, or rather, the ground is actually a very dull slaty-blue, over which are trailed the stems and leaves of the orange tree, with the rounded fruit in various sizes and stages of matu-rity, from the tender green to the warm orange-yellow. . . . The whole coloring, however, of this paper is so deli-ciously cool and subdued, that scarcely one thing stands

[12] Frank L. Smith, *Suburban Homes* (Boston: Wood, Harmon, and Co., 1890), 16.

out above another, so that it is some time before you grasp the whole of the design. . . . The entire effect is that of a quiet and comfortable, home-like room. . . . The whole thing, moreover, is in good taste, and any ruffled feelings which you might have had on entering must involuntarily be smoothed down before you have been seated ten minutes.[13]

Shoppell goes on to argue that, despite what by today's standards might appear to be rather complex and ornate decorations, the dining room should be supplied with "plain, substantial, and homely" kinds of furniture, restrained wall papers, and functional buffets. His emphasis on the unity of design and an aesthetic that praised art for art's sake was part of a redirection in American artistic standards between the

FIG. 14 *This illustration from* George O. Garnsey's National Builder's Album of Beautiful Homes, Villas, Residences and Cot tages *(1891) displays the elaborate shelving and sideboards now needed to contain the extra china, linens, and silverware for formal, multicourse meals. Courtesy Avery Architectural and Fine Arts Library, Columbia University.*

[13] Robert W. Shoppell, *How to Build, Furnish, and Decorate* (New York: Co-operative Building Plan Association, 1883), 6.

Clifford E. Clark, Jr.

[14] David C. Huntington, "The Quest for Unity: American Art between World's Fairs, 1876–1893," in Detroit Institute of Arts, *The Quest for Unity* (Chicago: Rohner Printing Co., 1983), 15. On the expositions' impact on sideboard design see Kenneth Ames, "The Battle of the Sideboards," *Winterthur Portfolio* 9 (1974): 1–27.
[15] On the feminist reformers, see Dolores Hayden, *The Grand Domestic Revolution: A History of Feminist Designs for American Homes, Neighborhoods, and Cities* (Cambridge: M.I.T. Press, 1981), 1–21, 150–70; on the contrary claims of reformers, builders, and developers, see Gwendolyn Wright, *Moralism and the Model Home* (Chicago: University of Chicago Press, 1980).

1876 Philadelphia Centennial Exhibition and the 1893 World's Columbian Exposition. Art historian David C. Huntington has called this shift "a quest for unity." The American public, tired of the emphasis that painting and sculpture placed on moralistic themes and confused by the welter of different styles for machine-made furniture, began to search for art that expressed the creativity of the individual person and that took as its subject the everyday and the commonplace. Hence the fascination with Japanese art with its clean lines and its delineation of ordinary events. As Huntington has suggested, "While ideas essentially literary in nature might sustain painting and sculpture, such ideas could not have been expected to sustain with equal success the so-called applied arts. It is perhaps for this very reason that discontent with the state of American decorative arts was willingly voiced. In 1876 the need for reform was sensed much more keenly in the realm of household art than in the 'fine' arts. That household art should have proved to be the catalyst in the quest for discipline in design is, surely, one of the distinctive consequences of the Centennial Exhibition."[14] Household art represented by glass, silverware, and pottery as well as by lace work, doilies, painted trays, and sugar sculptures seemed an ideal medium in which to fuse the useful with the distinctive.

The importance of the house as a work of art was not the only theme stressed by architects and plan book writers in the 1880s. The other major concern was to make running the house more efficient and economical. Food preparation and mealtime activities, always a concern because of the amount of time and energy invested in them, now became a center of attention. Where radical feminists such as M.I.T. chemist Ellen Swallow Richards and trade union leader Mary Kenney urged the creation of cooperative housekeeping in hotels or apartment complexes that had central kitchens, moderate reformers tried to make the conventional middle-class kitchen and dining room more efficient.[15] Catering to the interest in more economical homes, architect Louis H. Gibson argued in his 1889 plan book, *Convenient Houses,* that careful planning would make housekeeping easier. The average housekeeper, he asserted, was overworked. Starting early in the morning, the housekeeper had to warm up the house, kindle the kitchen fire, dress the children, cook and serve breakfast, and start the washing. Then came washing the breakfast dishes, getting the children off to school, making the beds, ordering grocery and butcher supplies—whether from the boy who called at the door or by visiting the stores—setting the dining room table, and starting to cook dinner, which was usually served at noon. Afternoons were spent with more dishes, more washing, cooking supper, taking care of the children when they came home from school, tending the fires, and carrying out the ashes. Evenings might be somewhat more restful, but still there was mending and darning to be done in addition to crocheting and other "fancy work."

Given this hectic daily schedule, Gibson suggested that the dining room have certain practical features: it should be at least thirteen feet wide and fifteen feet long (a size suggested to accommodate the rectangular or oval table), with a pass-through pantry, a high window, and a sideboard placed at the end of the room nearest the entrance to the kitchen and the china closet. He was particularly insistent about having a good sideboard. "The sideboard has various uses, according to the plans of the housekeeper," he explained. "In some cases it is merely a place to display dainty china and other table furniture. Below are places for linen and table cutlery. In other cases, the sideboard is used as a buffet; as a place from which to serve food. Sometimes this is carried to the extremist degree, and includes the carving, and the serving which goes with meats" (fig. 15).[16]

Not content with simply pointing out the functional features of the dining room, Gibson went on to stress the artistic potential of the room, arguing that a beautiful house not only gave pleasure to all who saw it, but was also a source of education to the occupants, serving to "lift them from that which is common

[16] Louis H. Gibson, *Convenient Houses, with Fifty Plans for the Housekeeper* (New York: Thomas Y. Crowell and Co., 1889), 38.

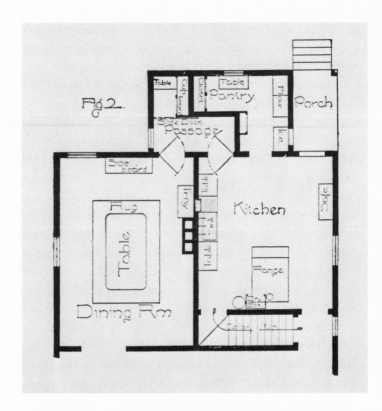

FIG. 15 *Louis Gibson's design for a kitchen and the adjoining dining room, taken from his plan book* Convenient Houses *(New York: Thomas Y. Crowell and Co., 1889), demonstrated the concern with the careful planning that was necessary to make serving meals easier.*

and ordinary." Because the dining room served as the place of assembly for the family, it was usually the only room where the family as a whole regularly spent time together. Hence it was to be attractive and restful, with a place for plants and flowers, a high shelf that might serve for the display of cups, an attractive sideboard, a coloring somewhat richer and heavier than the rest of the house, and, as a special feature, a built-in china cabinet, which had doors both front and back that would open into the dining room and into the pantry. Thus, even those accounts which emphasized function also stressed the importance of the house as a work of art. As Gibson put it, "People may be surrounded by that which is beautiful and artistic, and for a time fail to realize its true excellence, or they may be surrounded with that which is homely and crude without knowing the full measure of its ugliness. The time must come, however, when the truth will be realized to a certain extent. If it is in the direction of the appreciation of what is beautiful, it must necessarily bring about a higher state of mind."[17]

Given the widespread publication of authoritative plan books such as Gibson's and the power of the vision of the house as a work of art, the question remains of what impact these books had on middle-class decoration and furnishing of the dining room. Although evidence can only be gathered in a somewhat impressionistic fashion from family letters and photographs that survive, it is clear that many middle-class Americans tried to uphold the dining room ideals set forth in the plan and advice books and tried to follow their decorating suggestions. When the family had some money, as did that of St. Paul, Minnesota, lawyer Henry James, there was a clear attempt to make the house into a work of art. Writing to her aunt, Mrs. Frances Linda James delighted in describing the decorations in her new house built in 1888. "The parlor is lovely," she commented, "ceiling pale cream, frieze pale olive ending a foot from the ceiling, walls dull olive, woodwork natural pine which is a beautiful soft yellow." Her mother, who visited often, wrote to Mrs. James's aunt and stressed the beauty of the rooms. "I am sitting in our lovely dining room," she said, "the sun streaming in every window into a room with a delightful atmosphere." It was a big house, she commented in another letter that same year, and at a recent dinner party "the table was just as dainty as could be. First course, sweetbreads with delicate potatoes. Second, sweet peas and what goes with them—and chocolate. Third, ice cream and cake."[18]

That even lower middle-class clerks aspired to have an elaborate dining room can be seen in the example of Walter Teller Post (fig. 16). Born in Michigan, Post moved to St. Paul in the 1890s and took a position as a junior clerk for the Northern Pacific Railway. Shortly thereafter, he married Ulilla "Lillie" Carl of Peru, Indiana. In long detailed letters to his father, Post listed their wedding gifts, including a half-dozen silver fruit knives, a half-dozen oyster forks, a gravy ladle,

[17] Ibid., 86–98.
[18] Frances Linda James to Helen Neil Jaynes, 29 February 1888; Harriet Williams to Helen Neil Jaynes, 21 March 1888 and 30 June 1888; in Frances Haynes James and Family Papers, Minnesota Historical Society. For an excellent introduction to this material see Joan M. Seidl, "Consumers' Choices: A Study of Household Furnishing, 1880–1920," *Minnesota History* 48, no. 5 (Spring 1983): 183–97.

Clifford E. Clark, Jr.

FIG. 16 *Walter Teller Post*
(1867–1930) in March 1893.
Photograph by Harry Shepherd,
St. Paul, Minnesota. Courtesy Post
Papers, Minnesota Historical
Society.

a carving set, four sugar bowls and creamers, a half-dozen Haviland China plates, a half-dozen glasses, a half-dozen silver teaspoons "from home," books, a framed picture, and a stick pin. Two weeks after his marriage, he decided to rent a house, explaining to his father that the $18 that he paid for a six-room house with gas and bath was a better buy than trying to rent an apartment. To furnish the house, Post spent $150 at Schuneman and Evans' department store, paying $100 down and promising to pay the rest in sixty days.

Dutifully, as if expecting his father's censure of his extravagances, Post explained his purchases and drew a diagram of his house, complete with stick figures of himself and his wife in the

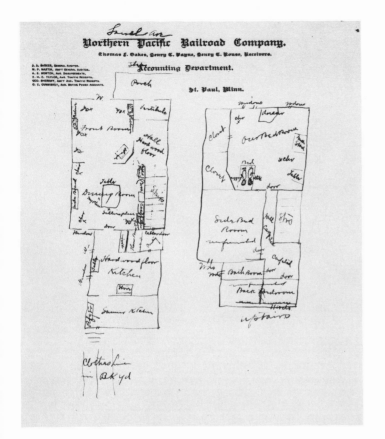

FIG. 17 *Walter Teller Post sent this drawing of the placement of the new furniture in his house to his father. 9 August 1894. Courtesy Post Papers, Minnesota Historical Society.*

upstairs bed (fig. 17). In each room of the house, he commented, they had purchased the bare minimum. For the front room, he bought only rocking chairs—"a handsome polished & carved oak $7.25, a Rattan 4.95 [,] 1 upholstered $3.95. . . . In our dining room," he added, "will be one dining table. $13.50 solid quarter sawed oak. 1 side board $19.50, 4 dining chairs $5.00." It is significant that the furniture for the dining room, especially the sideboard, was the most expensive in the whole house, demonstrating the importance of the dining room for the self-image of the middle class.[19]

Although Walter Post, as historian Joan Seidl has pointed out, "clung to the bottommost rung of the middle-class lad-

[19] Walter Teller Post to his father, 3, 20, and 27 July and 9 August 1894. Walter Teller Post Papers, Minnesota Historical Society.

Clifford E. Clark, Jr.

der," eventually defaulted to the department store on the pay-
ment for his furniture, and was forced to move into a flat, his
experience demonstrates the importance of the dining room in
the middle-class definition of respectability.

Although the evidence from family correspondence is scat-
tered, photographs taken by families who were proud enough
of their decorative endeavors to record them are certain proof
of the power of the plan books' decorative ideals. A typical
home was that of Dr. Russell Berthel on Portland Avenue in
St. Paul, Minnesota (fig. 18). The sun streaming in the partially
closed blinds in the picture indicates that the dining room, as
the plan books suggested, was oriented on a southeastern
exposure. The light-colored wallpaper with the simple frieze at
the top fit well with the classical urn pedestal to give the room
the relatively clean lines that were admired by plan book
authors. The plants, together with the pictures of hunting dogs
and the fruit on the sideboard, created a unity of design around
the food motif, one that the plan books viewed as appropriate

FIG. 19 *The use of plants as a window decoration in the Berthel residence followed the advice offered in Beecher and Stowe's* American Woman's Home.

for the dining room. Although the elaborate plates on the sideboard and the silver baskets on the table created a somewhat formal atmosphere, that feeling was counterbalanced by the highchair, with its bib, at the table. Following the suggestions that Catharine Beecher and Harriet Beecher Stowe had made in *The American Woman's Home,* the bay window was decorated with ferns and trailing ivy, softening the lines of the room (fig. 19). This is clearly a room for the family as well as for guests.

Similar themes can be found in the photographs of the dining rooms in the Alexander Robertson house in St. Paul, Minnesota, the J. W. Andrews home in Mankato, Minnesota, and the Charles Betcher residence in Red Wing, Minnesota (figs. 20, 21, and 22). All the dining rooms were decorated with light-colored wallpapers. The Robertson room with its flight of ducks followed the outdoors theme that was seen in the Berthel dining room. The Betcher and the Andrews dining rooms also present a floral theme, one with the symmetrical flower pictures on the walls and the other with the picture over the fireplace and the floral-patterned carpet. Even though the amount of china and silver in each clearly reflects quite different income levels, all four rooms used the ever-present sideboard to display china and silver.

To argue that these rooms represent some of the prominent ideals presented in the pattern books is not to say, however, that they represent a slavish adherence to the advice. In the Andrews home, the sideboard blocked the window, contrary to the advice offered in the plan books. Although the same problem did not occur in the Theodore Hamm residence in St. Paul, Minnesota, the size and elaborate nature of the sideboard overpowered one end of the room (fig. 23). Nor did every middle-class household choose lighter-colored wallpapers or the pastel colors argued for in the plan books. The dining room in the Ferdinand Hinrich home in St. Paul and in the J. F. Williams home in Chicago were darker and more cluttered with china (figs. 24 and 25). Nevertheless, they too reveal a new preoccupation with decorating the dining room in a way carefully contrived to create an artistic effect.

By the 1890s the vast plan book and magazine literature had become both a reflection of and an influence on middle-class

The Vision of the Dining Room

FIGS. 20, 21, and 22 *The dining rooms in the Alexander Robertson house in St. Paul (ca. 1900), the Charles Betcher home in Red Wing, Minnesota, and the J. W. Andrews residence in Mankato (ca. 1890), similarly evinced their owners' interests in light-colored walls. Photographs courtesy Minnesota Historical Society.*

FIG. 23 *A massive sideboard dominated the dining room in Theodore Hamm's residence in St. Paul, Minnesota. Photograph, ca. 1890, Northwestern Photo Co., St. Paul, courtesy Minnesota Historical Society.*

FIG. 24 *This torn photographic view of the Ferdinand Hinrich home on East Fifth Street in St. Paul (ca. 1904) demonstrates the visual continuity in design between the dining room and the parlor. Photograph courtesy Minnesota Historical Society.*

FIG. 25 *The dining room in the home of Dr. J. F. Williams in Chicago (ca. 1902) prominently displayed his collection of silver and china. Photograph courtesy Minnesota Historical Society.*

dining room decoration. The advice literature publicized a set of decorative ideals and provided examples that the middle class could follow. Because an important component of having an "artistic" house was the opportunity it offered to express one's individuality in the layout and furnishings of the room, middle-class Americans were encouraged to create—with the aid of considerable advice—distinctive dining rooms. The growing availability of new furnishings and decorative materials allowed individual families to create their "own" rooms and yet remain within the general artistic guidelines prescribed by the plan books. What is clear from the letters and pictures that survive from the 1880s and 1890s is that, following the lead of the magazine and plan book promoters, the dining room had become a central symbol for the attainment of middle-class status. Linen, silver, and china which accompanied elaborate meals and stylized dining room etiquette were now widely accepted as signs of having entered the ranks of the middle-class consumer society. Even poor immigrants, much to the disgust of social reformers in Boston who urged them to adopt the slow-cooking Aladdin oven and eat stews, rejected the reformers' vision; instead, they continued to demonstrate

Clifford E. Clark, Jr.

their conviction that one of the marks of success in America was eating a roast of beef or a steak.[20] The letters of Walter Post, a man who was one step higher in the lower managerial ranks of a large corporation, revealed his pride in the decoration of his dining room. Although the front parlor still remained an important public space, the dining room had now come to represent the realization of artistic creativity, good breeding, and hospitality: only those whose jobs were secure and whose good taste was unquestioned could afford to enjoy an elaborate, multicourse meal, complemented by fine linens and silver. For them, a space earlier regarded as safe harbor for the family had been transformed into a showcase of middle-class accomplishment.

[20] Harvey Levenstein, "The New England Kitchen and the Origins of Modern American Eating Habits," *American Quarterly* 32, no. 4 (Fall 1980): 369–86.

Victorian Dining Silver

DOROTHY RAINWATER

OLD and silver have long been used to express the power and wealth of upper classes in Western societies. During the eighteenth century, when most members of the middle classes in Britain and the United States were using pewter vessels and utensils at their dining tables, more prosperous families considered it fashionable to establish a permanent record of their means by having their portrait painted around a table on which the family silver service was shown in use.

It was not until the middle of the nineteenth century that the burgeoning American middle class was similarly able to express its rising status through the acquisition of silver tablewares (fig. 1). Although a form of plated silver tablewares had been made in England since the 1720s, the coincidence of a number of events in the years just before the Civil War made silverplate widely available to people with moderate incomes.

The primary event was the discovery of an electrolytic method of depositing silver on less expensive base metals. As

early as 1801, English experiments had determined that electricity could collect or disperse atoms of pure silver in solution and direct them onto other metals. Between 1836 and 1838 the British firm of G. R. and A. Elkington took out numerous patents for the process, and by the latter year Elkington was electroplating buttons. By the 1840s, other English firms, centered around the city of Sheffield, were electroplating tablewares and exporting them to the United States.

Nineteenth-century silverplate differs from eighteenth-century Sheffield plate in significant ways. Sheffield plate was formed in a thermomechanical process, not an electrical one; two or more ingots of silver and copper were bound together with a small amount of borax and then heated in a furnace until the precise moment of their fusion. The plate was then cooled, cleaned, hammered, and rolled to the desired shape and thickness and is in fact a "sandwich" of the two metals. Objects made of Sheffield plate were thus formed after plating; the forms of electroplated wares are fashioned before the plating process takes place (fig. 2).

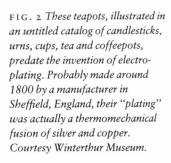

FIG. 2 *These teapots, illustrated in an untitled catalog of candlesticks, urns, cups, tea and coffeepots, predate the invention of electroplating. Probably made around 1800 by a manufacturer in Sheffield, England, their "plating" was actually a thermomechanical fusion of silver and copper. Courtesy Winterthur Museum.*

By the 1840s, various manufacturers in New England had begun to manufacture silverplate. Asa Rogers, Jr., and two other Connecticut men were making and selling silverplated spoons in considerable quantities by 1844. Two other major silverplate manufacturers had begun business making britannia, a compound of tin, copper, and antimony that was harder and more lustrous than pewter and served as the chief base metal in the early years of electroplating. After 1852, six

Dorothy Rainwater

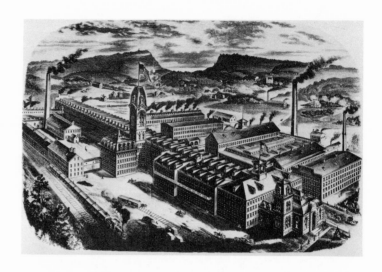

FIG. 3 *Meriden Britannia Company, created by the combination of several Connecticut britannia ware manufacturers, included this view of its West Meriden, Conn., factory—a vision of prosperity—in its 1879 catalog.*

or seven Connecticut britannia makers combined into the Meriden Britannia Company, which by 1867 was advertising silverplate as having "all the advantages of silver in desirability and beauty at one-fifth the cost" (fig. 3). By 1848, the firm of Reed and Barton of Taunton, Massachusetts, had turned its attention to silverplated ware, having begun to make britannia ware under the name of Babbit and Crossman as early as 1824.

The American silverplate industry was greatly aided in its early years by the passage of a protective tariff. In 1842 a number of New York silversmiths met with Henry Clay in Washington to discuss the tariff; Clay's efforts were instrumental in the passage of the act in August of that same year. The tariff levied a duty of 30 percent on all importations of gold and silverware, whether solid or plated.

Still, the development of affordable silverplate awaited an abundant supply, which was soon forthcoming. New ore deposits were accidentally discovered, the most important being the colossal Comstock Silver Lode on the eastern slope of Mount Davidson in Nevada in 1859, which shortly made the United States the largest producer of silver in the world. From the nineteenth century, the principal consumer of silver had been the silverware industry.

Later discoveries of silver deposits in Mexico, Australia, and elsewhere greatly increased the amount of available silver while lowering its cost. Improved industrial processes and the invention of new machinery also made it possible to mass produce tablewares previously only produced by tedious hand labor. Making dies for original patterns was an expensive process; the earliest patterns available in the United States were produced from blanks made in England and brought to this country for plating. Manufacturers openly copied English designs in the 1830s and 1840s, but by the late 1850s new types of decoration began to appear. In 1852, Reed and Barton hired its first chaser (chasing is a form of decoration worked into the surface of a piece, similar to engraving except that no metal is removed), and after that date incised floral patterns appeared on its tablewares. Engine turning (a type of machine engraving) also became popular. Before 1860, when Reed and Barton installed its own lathe, the company sent some of its wares to Boston to be decorated with geometric patterns (fig. 4).

The development of the ability to stamp and raise flatware patterns by machine (an event that cannot be precisely dated) encouraged the proliferation of silverplated tableware patterns as well as their elaborate ornamentation. The use of shaped dies for flatware made possible the production of thousands of identical pieces and also stimulated the development of a multiplicity of types of pieces in a single pattern (fig. 5).

The trend toward variety in design started early among flatware manufacturers. The first patented American flatware pattern, which I call "Gibney I" for its New York silver designer, Michael Gibney, was patented on 4 December 1844. Most early silverplated flatware of this period was modeled after traditional designs. In 1847 Rogers Brothers made silverplated flatware in only three patterns, "Plain," "Threaded," and "Tipped"; in 1848 the company added flatware in the "Olive" pattern, which is believed to be the first fancy pattern made in this country. Patterns of the 1840s usually featured spoons

FIG. 4 *In its 12 May 1877 issue,*
Scientific American *featured a*
drawing of a stamped die for flat-
ware on its cover. The design for
this pattern of fork was engraved
directly into a steel roll; the roll was
then rotated on a machine against a
"blank" of silver or white metal.
Courtesy University of Rochester
Library.

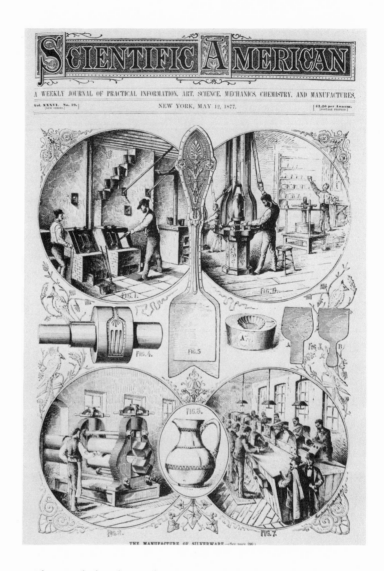

with rounded ends. By the 1850s, some ends of the spoons were pointed, and more designs were introduced. In the 1860s, designs began to appear for the first time above the halfway mark of the spoon handle. Spoons of the 1870s became more angular, and with the invention of machinery that could make deeper impressions on flatware, patterns appeared that were more deeply stamped. In the 1880s and 1890s, replicas of

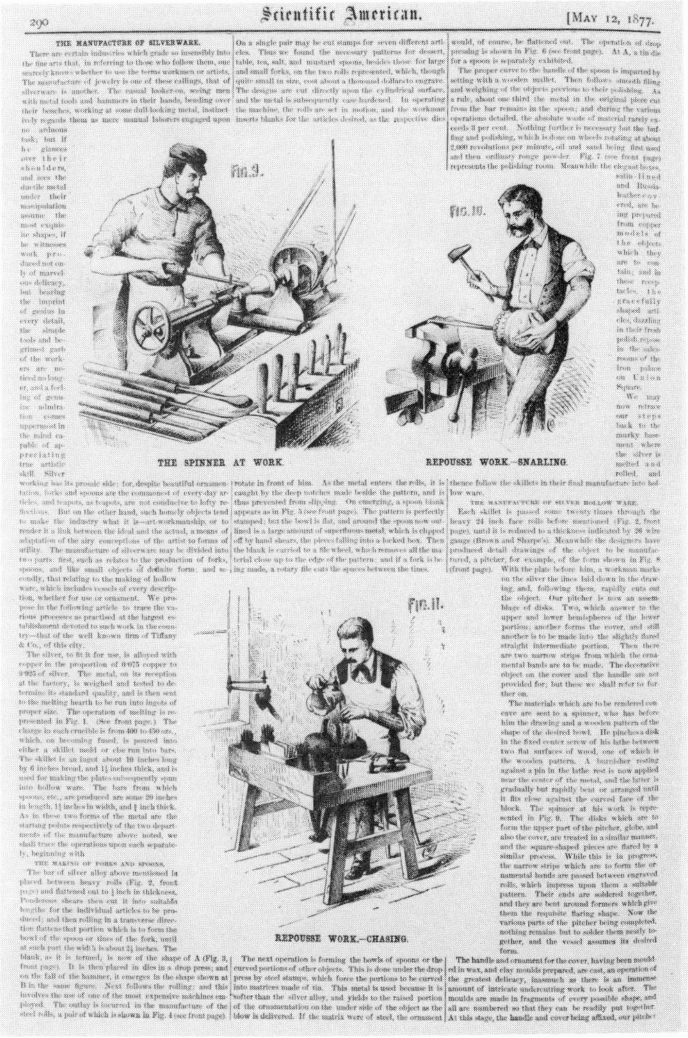

THE SPINNER AT WORK   REPOUSSE WORK.—SNARLING.

REPOUSSE WORK.—CHASING.

FIG. 5 *The 1877* Scientific American *article described and illustrated the machine processes involved in the manufacture of silver flatware and holloware as practiced by Tiffany and Company of New York City. Though Tiffany made wares of sterling silver, silverplate manufacturers used many of the same processes. Repoussé, meaning "repulsed" or "pushed back," is a technique that involves hammering on an object from within, denting it outward in a decorative fashion; the magazine called it "probably the highest branch of the silversmith's art," and it was used to decorate both sterling and silverplate.* Scientific American *called the silverware industry "art-workmanship . . . a means of adaptation of the airy conceptions of the artist to the form of utility," and praised Tiffany for "directly educating men as art workers" at a time when "art museums and similar means of educating popular tastes are few and far between" in the United States. Courtesy University of Rochester Library.*

human figures began to be designed into flatware, and handles became much more elaborate.

Early silverplate catalogs simply list available tablewares with no illustration. An 1855 catalog of the Rogers Brothers, which until the late 1860s probably produced most of the flatware blanks plated and stamped by other American manufacturers, listed teaspoons, coffee spoons, dessert spoons, salt

Dorothy Rainwater

FIG. 6a–c *The Towle Company's
"Georgian" pattern, introduced in
1898, included 131 separate eating
and serving utensils, helping to
bring the proliferation of specialized flatware forms to a crescendo
by the end of the century. The 1898
catalog depicted an array of
spoons, forks, tongs, and servers
offered in the pattern (here, they are
reproduced at 27 percent of their
actual size). Courtesy
Donald Soeffing.*

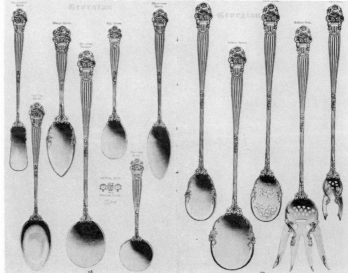

spoons, and tablespoons, forks in two sizes, dessert forks,
table knives, dessert knives, sugar shells, asparagus tongs, and
ice tongs. The 1856 catalog of the E. Jaccard Company of
St. Louis, Missouri, featured flatware in a Rogers Brothers
pattern (which was almost certainly produced by Rogers

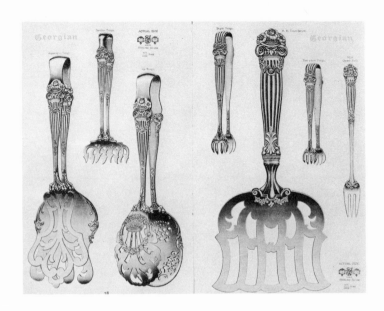

Brothers); within one year, bar spoons, egg spoons, oyster forks, pickle forks, mustard spoons, sugar shovels, sugar tongs, jelly spoons, soup spoons, crumb knives, cream ladles, and gravy ladles had been added to the service.

Many new kinds of serving pieces were also added in the 1880s and 1890s. By 1900, Rogers Brothers had introduced fifty-one flatware patterns, twenty-seven of them in the twenty years between 1880 and 1900. Many of these have had remarkably long life spans, but the numbers of new patterns introduced in a single decade were never as high as they had been in the 1880s and 1890s. The number of types of pieces produced in any one pattern also declined after the 1890s.

Sterling silver manufacturers did not produce catalogs at a very early date, but a few jewelers' catalogs have survived. The 1856 E. Jaccard Company catalog offered thirty-four different pieces of flatware in thirteen patterns; identical patterns were offered in solid silver and silverplate. By 1870, Bailey and Company of Philadelphia (now Bailey, Banks and Biddle) offered sixty to seventy items in its sterling patterns. By 1898, the Towle Company's "Georgian" pattern included 131 different

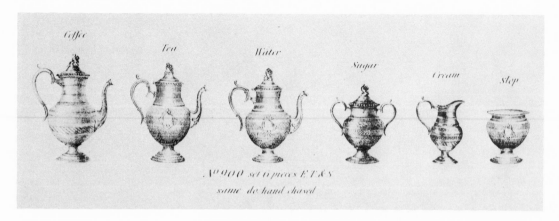

Coffee · Tea · Water · Sugar · Cream · Slop

N° 900 set 6 pieces E.T.&S
same do. hand chased

FIG. 7 *This illustration in the 1868 catalog of J. F. Curran and Company presented the component parts of a tea service—a coffeepot, teapot, hot water kettle, a sugar bowl and creamer, and a "slop" bowl for cold tea—as well as the company's selection of decorative finishes, such as engine turned, satin, and hand chased.*

pieces; to form a complete service for twelve in this pattern, one would have had to purchase 1,888 pieces. There were nineteen types of spoons for conveying food to the mouth, seventeen for serving, ten pieces for serving and carving, six ladles, and twenty-seven pieces for serving that were not classified as ladles, forks, or spoons. One can sympathize with the hostess of that day in trying to be sure that croquettes were not served with a patty server, or cucumbers with a tomato server (fig. 6a–c).

In 1907 Reed and Barton introduced its "Francis I" pattern as "The World's Most Complete Sterling Service," though it was not as diversified as Towle's "Georgian" pattern. Seventy-seven individual items were offered, most of them still available until very recently. And although the general trend seems to have been toward the simplification of flatware services, in 1926 some patterns were still being made in as many as 146 different pieces. Today, it is a rare design in which more than twenty different items can be found.

Aside from flatware, a complete tea and coffee service was probably the most essential kind of tableware. Because tea and coffee drinking were important elements in a family's hospitality, a tea service was part of any well-furnished household. Most sets included two or three pots (for coffee, tea, and often hot water), a sugar bowl, a creamer, and a waste bowl (fig. 7). It

FIG. 8 *The whimsical naturalism of the rococo style, which originally flourished during the mid-eighteenth century, is evident in the pear-shaped body, rustic handles, leaf and berry finial, and general foliate decoration of this silver-plated coffee urn, a rococo revival example made about 1855.*

was possible also to buy matching pieces, such as swing kettles for hot water, coffee urns, spoon holders, butter dishes, cake baskets, syrup pitchers, and trays, both to augment the tea table and to display on the sideboard.

Because of their popularity, silverplated tea services may be used to trace the development of design in tablewares from the

Dorothy Rainwater

FIG. 9 *Raised and cast flowers, acanthus leaves, C-scrolls, and other naturalistic elements dominate the decoration of this rococo revival teapot, made sometime during the third quarter of the nineteenth century. Its repoussé views of Mount Vernon and Washington's tomb, along with the eagle finial, suggest a connection with the American Centennial, celebrated in 1876.*

beginnings of electroplating forward. Although some of the earliest Victorian tea and coffee services were based on simple classical shapes such as urns, others were highly ornamented. In the 1840s there was evidence of a revival of the rococo style which had been popular just before the American Revolution. By 1850 the rococo revival was in full swing (fig. 8). The style made heavy use of naturalistic motifs; vessels were leaf-shaped with rustic twigs and grapevines for handles, and acorns, grapes, birds, or animals for finials. Shapes were also naturalistic; curved lines were often exaggerated, and the pear and inverted-pear shapes of the eighteenth-century rococo style prevailed (fig. 9).

The rococo revival lasted well into the 1860s. From about 1865 until 1900, American silver reflected wide popular inter-

est in numerous historical styles and exotic cultures (fig. 10). There were revivals of neoclassical, rococo, and Italian Renaissance, Elizabethan, Egyptian, Persian, Jacobean, Japanese, Etruscan, and Moorish motifs. Tea sets of the 1870s are easily identified by a "long-legged" look, angular handles, and a diversity of cast, stamped, chased, and engraved ornamentation. Decorative bands adapted from Greek and Roman friezes were applied to all sorts of vessels. Designs often combined numerous motifs, borrowed from widely ranging sources. Dolphins, birds, cows, dogs, lions, sphinxes, animal paws, and winged cupids served as supports and finials; straight-sided vessels were engraved and chased with designs of flowers, butterflies, birds, and geometrics. Also in the 1870s, coffeepots began to be noticeably larger, more elongated, and longer-necked than teapots, showing the influence of Turkish and Persian designs.

By the 1880s and 1890s, tea services showed a trend away from the tall look and became squatter; some rested on a low rim or on small, curved feet. The high flaring collars on some 1870s services had virtually disappeared by the 1880s, and footed wares were less frequently introduced. Ornamentation was often simpler, too. No one style completely replaced any others, and several styles sometimes existed side by side on the same ornamented piece.

Art Nouveau, a style derived from elements of Japanese and pre-Raphaelite art, coexisted with motifs from Byzantine, Moorish, Egyptian, and Roman cultures. Although the Art Nouveau movement began in Europe in the 1880s, it did not

FIG. 10 *These teapots show a range of styles popular from the 1850s through the first decade of the twentieth century. At far left, the rococo revival silverplated teapot in the "Charter Oak" pattern has repoussé decorations of oak leaves and acorns and was advertised in the 1867 catalog of Rogers, Smith, and Company. The next teapot, made by Ball, Black and Company around 1870, shows the influence of the Egyptian revival in its pharaoh-head finial, the cobra-head spout, and the coptic motifs which appear as chased decoration around the neck. The machine-hammered teapot at center, made in the 1880s by Meriden Britannia Company, attempts to simulate the handwork of previous centuries, and also demonstrates a trend away from the "long-legged" look of teapots made in the 1870s. The sterling silver repoussé teapot by Gorham Manufacturing Company, made between 1881 and 1886, further illustrates the growing demand for luxury silverwares that exhibit a great deal of handwork in their decoration or fabrication. The complete tea set in this pattern cost $371 in 1881. Gorham's silverplated teapot of 1913–14 demonstrates the nation's interest in reviving colonial styles.*

Dorothy Rainwater

FIG. 11 *The sinuous lines of this tea set, manufactured by Derby Silver Company of Derby, Conn., around 1905, show the popularity of the European Art Nouveau style. Silver and fabrics, more than did furniture (which was much more expensive), bore the influence of the style in the United States.*

FIG. 12 *British designer William C. Codman designed the Martelé line for Gorham Corporation. This melon-shaped, sterling silver teapot with its repoussé design of meandering flowers, designed around 1900, was originally owned by Florence Hooker Cheney of Chicago. Martelé, which is French for "hand-hammered," combined an emphasis on hand craftsmanship, promulgated by the English Arts and Crafts movement, with the stylized naturalism of French Art Nouveau.*

influence silver design in the United States until close to the turn of the century, and it had a relatively short life here. It is easily identified by its free-flowing organic lines and was more often employed on bowls, small trays, and dresserware than it was on tea and coffee services. Art Nouveau was most successfully

FIG. 13 *This hand-hammered sugar and creamer set was made of silverplate by Derby Silver Company, then part of International Silver Company, between 1898 and 1933. In the Arts and Crafts style, the set emulated the craftsmanship of preindustrial silver manufacture; many tea wares made at this time achieved similar effects through machine hammering.*

executed in this country by William Christmas Codman, a British tableware designer brought to the United States by Gorham to direct its design department and train its designers in the new style (fig. 11). Gorham's first pieces in this style were placed on the market in 1901. This Martelé line was always expensive, however, and would not have been bought for most middle-class Victorian homes (fig. 12). At about the same time, tea services began to show the influence of the Arts and Crafts and Colonial Revival movements; some tea sets were hammered by machine in an attempt to approximate the hand-hammered sets of preindustrial times. The nationwide interest in colonial styles was a complete departure from the highly ornate forms of the previous several decades (fig. 13).

Tea and coffee services were more essential, but it might be argued that caster sets were more peculiarly Victorian. The caster set held containers for seasonings and condiments and was found in a prominent location in the center of most Victorian dinner tables, as well as in public dining rooms. Probably descended from the eighteenth-century frames made to hold glass oil and vinegar cruets and other condiments, caster sets became important articles in the trade of britannia makers by the 1840s. In 1834, the Taunton Britannia Company (the predecessor of Reed and Barton) shipped 410 casters,

FIG. 14 *By the 1840s, caster sets to hold seasonings and condiments had become important items in the stock-in-trade of American silverplate manufacturers. J. F. Curran offered ten styles of dinner casters in its 1868 catalog.*

FIG. 15 *In 1871 Meriden Britannia Company offered more than one hundred elaborate patterns, including this tall, globelike caster.*

which was little more than 8 percent of its total shipment; four years later, it shipped 7,416 caster frames, more than 40 percent of its shipment that year.

Early silverplated casters were usually set on low legs or on a relatively low, center pedestal. Around the base was a wide pierced band or one decorated with grape and 'eaf clusters. A

FIG. 16 *Casters of the 1880s were manufactured with such embellishments as egg cups, as was the one featured in the 1887 Simpson, Hall, Miller and Company catalog.*

FIG. 17 *The 1891 catalog of Simpson, Hall, Miller and Company showed a combination caster and fruit dish.*

FIG. 18 *By the turn of the century, the importance of casters began to diminish; the catalog of the International Silver Company of around 1900 showed one dinner caster, whose form was simplified in comparison to casters of the 1870s and 1880s.*

center handle projected upward for passing the caster at the table. Dinner casters were made by most of the major silverplate manufacturers from the beginning of electroplating. Meriden Britannia Company offered casters in 75 different patterns in 1861, and in 122 patterns by 1869. By the 1870s, casters, like tea sets, began to become taller; in its 1877 catalog,

FIG. 19 *This pickle caster was made by Homan Manufacturing Company of Cincinnati around 1890. The frame and tongs are silverplate; the caster is cranberry glass, molded in a thumbprint pattern and decorated with enameled sprays of flowers.*

Reed and Barton offered both four- and six-bottle casters on four legs or on rather tall pedestals. Revolving casters appeared, sometimes with call bells incorporated into heavily decorated handles. Casters were even taller in the 1880s, when bells, egg cups, and bouquet holders were sometimes added (figs. 14–18). In the 1880s, pickle casters also began to assume real importance, as silverplate manufacturers worked to design frames that would complement the cut and engraved glass bottles which held the condiments themselves (fig. 19).

FIG. 20 *As the practice of serving food from the sideboard, pantry, or kitchen instead of from bowls and platters on the table gained popularity, women turned their attention to elaborate table decorations of fruit and flowers. A well-furnished epergne, such as this one featured in the Simpson, Hall, Miller and Company 1891 catalog, would certainly have livened up the "snowy desert" of an empty white tablecloth. Thirty-one inches high, this epergne was expensive and represented the top of the factory-produced line.*

For special occasions, an epergne (a decorative holder for flowers and fruits) might have been favored as the centerpiece (fig. 20). By the 1890s dinner casters began to lose their centrality on middle-class dining tables even at ordinary meals. Fruit dishes, centerpieces, and berry bowls began to replace them around 1875. These bowls, now called "bride's baskets" or "bride's bowls" because they were reputedly the favorite gifts of brides-to-be, were usually identified in catalogs and advertisements as fruit baskets (meaning that they featured overhead handles) or fruit stands, berry dishes, or fruit bowls (which stood on pedestals) (fig. 21). Often made with inserts of cut, engraved, or pressed glass, bride's baskets of the 1860s

Dorothy Rainwater

FIG. 21 *Many silver manufacturers teamed up with glass companies to produce an artistic product, such as this fruit or bride's bowl, made in 1856 of cased and enameled glass on a silverplated stand by Taunton Silverplate Company of Taunton, Mass. Its decorative details show the influence of both Gothic and Renaissance revivals.*

were decorated with beading, applied continuous bands in Greek key, and other relatively plain designs; sculptured human heads, lion masks, deer's and ram's heads also appeared on some, but even these were most austere compared to the elaborate creations of a decade later. One 1871 berry dish featured two female heads mounted around the glass, in much the manner of ships' figureheads. The frame rested on four hoofed feet between which was an Egyptian sphinx (made popular by Napoleon's Egyptian campaign). A full range of ornament—Greek and Roman medallions, swans, cherubs playing harps, mythological birds and animals, caryatids (columns sculpted in the form of women), floral swags, children playing with butterflies, turtles, lions draped with floral swags, water lilies and other floral motifs—was used on fruit stands, fruit dishes, and preserve dishes of the mid-1870s. And,

FIG. 22 *This bride's basket of the 1870s followed the trend of other tablewares of the time; instead of being supported by a pedestal, it rose up on legs. The butterfly, hummingbird, stylized flowers, and branches show a new American interest in Japanese design that had just begun to appear on many interior accessories and furnishings. The basket handles simulated bamboo in the same spirit, but the legs were cast and decorated in Renaissance revival style. This model was featured in Meriden Britannia Company's 1871 catalog.*

FIG. 23 *By the middle of the 1880s, the glass inserts of fruit stands had ruffled or fluted edges, and silverplate manufacturers created many styles of stands to support them. This fruit dish appeared in the 1891 catalog of Simpson, Hall, Miller and Company.*

just as teapots and coffeepots had risen up on high supports, so did many of the fruit stands. As rapidly as craftsmen working with art glass created and patented new glasswares in the 1880s, silverplate manufacturers created a wide variety of mounts and stands to enhance them (fig. 22).

FIGS. 24–29 *The round form of nineteenth-century pounds of butter gave butter dishes their distinctive shape. Fairly simple in design and low to the table in the 1850s and 1860s, as the "butter dishes or coolers" in the 1868 J. F. Curran catalog demonstrate (fig. 24), butter dishes began to rise up on legs in the 1870s, as does this from the 1871 Meriden Britannia catalog (fig. 25). Intricate mechanisms for raising the cover without having to remove it entirely began to appear in Meriden Britannia's 1879 catalog (fig. 26), and later butter dishes also demonstrate the society's interest in patented goods. Simpson, Hall, Miller and Company's 1887 catalog showed intricately decorated butter dishes (fig. 27), and, by the time its 1891 catalog was issued, the company featured a chased satin model "with patent revolving cover" and an illustration of how the butter dish opened (fig. 28). After the turn of the century, butter dishes reflected the tendency to simplify tablewares, as the model from the Eureka Silver Company catalog of about 1905 shows (fig. 29).*

About the middle of the 1880s, fruit stands with glass inserts that had ruffled or fluted edges appeared in silver manufacturers' catalogs. These bowls were produced in great number throughout the 1890s and long after the turn of the century, when their popularity—and that of other elaborate "fancy wares"—declined (fig. 23).

As the development of fruit baskets and bowls was stimulated by developments in the glass industry, the development of butter dishes was stimulated by the more mundane nineteenth-century methods of making butter. Until the rise of commercially produced creamery butter, much butter was made at home and molded in wooden butter molds or "prints" which usually held a pound. Butter prints were for the most part round and cup-shaped, and it was the need to accommodate these one-pound "prints" that gave the butter dish its shape and size.

Brittania butter dishes were being made as early as 1855, but, with the rapid advance of electroplating, silverplated butter dishes were produced in great quantities by the 1880s. In 1867 the Meriden Britannia Company catalog featured three pages of butter dishes, some designed to match tea services. Butter dishes often had compartments to hold ice to keep the butter cool, and they almost always had covers to keep flies away. Many covers were simply removed and placed on the table, but some butter dishes featured covers that could be hung from an arched handle over the dish; others "revolved" on pins, so that by turning the handle, the cover rolled under the base (figs. 24–30).

Another highly popular form on the Victorian dinner table was the cake basket, used to serve cakes or cookies at tea and dessert tables from the eighteenth century on. The low, footed cake baskets of the 1850s derived their shape and decoration largely from Sheffield plate baskets of twenty to thirty years earlier (fig. 31). In the United States, these baskets sat on slightly taller pedestals than English forms, and their handles tended to be a bit more ornamental; clusters of grapes similar

FIG. 30 *J. F. Curran's 1868 catalog featured an engraving of a butter dish with its "magic" revolving cover.*

Dorothy Rainwater

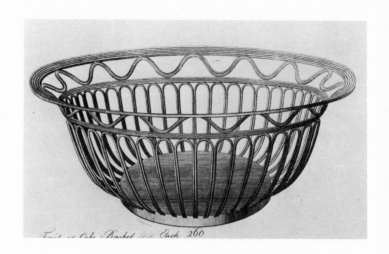

FIG. 3 1 *This "fruit or cake basket" from an undated catalog of silverplated ware, probably from a Sheffield, England, company, was used at tea and dessert tables. Its low oval form set the style of electroplated cake baskets after 1850. Courtesy Winterthur Museum.*

in style to those on tea and coffee services of the same period appeared on handles as well as on borders. Through the 1860s, cake baskets remained the same in form and decoration, often ornamented with applied medallions, engraving and chasing in floral designs, embossing, engine turning, and Greek key motifs. Different types of feet were fashioned for variety in decoration on footed baskets.

Cake baskets of the 1870s tended to have straighter lines and were often decorated with cast figures. As did other forms, cake baskets began to sport long legs in the 1870s, at which time they were also frequently ornamented in Egyptian motifs. Diversity of style marked the cake baskets that appeared around 1880; some were heavily ornamented, but a greater number were round baskets with overhead or bail-type handles having formal Renaissance detail such as continuous applied, geometric, floral (and, more rarely, scenic) borders. In 1885, Reed and Barton devoted sixteen pages of its catalog to the illustration of 118 different styles of cake baskets. New designs of the 1890s were set on shorter legs or on a single pedestal support. These new designs were frequently more restrained in their execution, although the exuberant patterns of the 1870s and 1880s continued to be offered by silverplate manufacturers, as catalogs document (figs. 32–36).

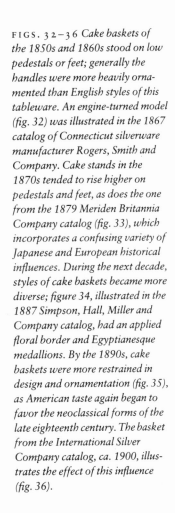

FIGS. 3 2 – 3 6 *Cake baskets of the 1850s and 1860s stood on low pedestals or feet; generally the handles were more heavily ornamented than English styles of this tableware. An engine-turned model (fig. 32) was illustrated in the 1867 catalog of Connecticut silverware manufacturer Rogers, Smith and Company. Cake stands in the 1870s tended to rise higher on pedestals and feet, as does the one from the 1879 Meriden Britannia Company catalog (fig. 33), which incorporates a confusing variety of Japanese and European historical influences. During the next decade, styles of cake baskets became more diverse; figure 34, illustrated in the 1887 Simpson, Hall, Miller and Company catalog, had an applied floral border and Egyptianesque medallions. By the 1890s, cake baskets were more restrained in design and ornamentation (fig. 35), as American taste again began to favor the neoclassical forms of the late eighteenth century. The basket from the International Silver Company catalog, ca. 1900, illustrates the effect of this influence (fig. 36).*

Another essential feature of every Victorian dining table, particularly at family meals, was napkin rings. Napkin rings are said to have been derived from fourteenth-century "nefs," silver and silver-gilt vessels in the form of sailing ships in which the napkins, knives, and other table utensils of royalty or nobility were kept. At that time, napkins were essentially towels, far larger than what we now use, and were brought to the table after the frequent washings that took place during meals eaten chiefly with the fingers.

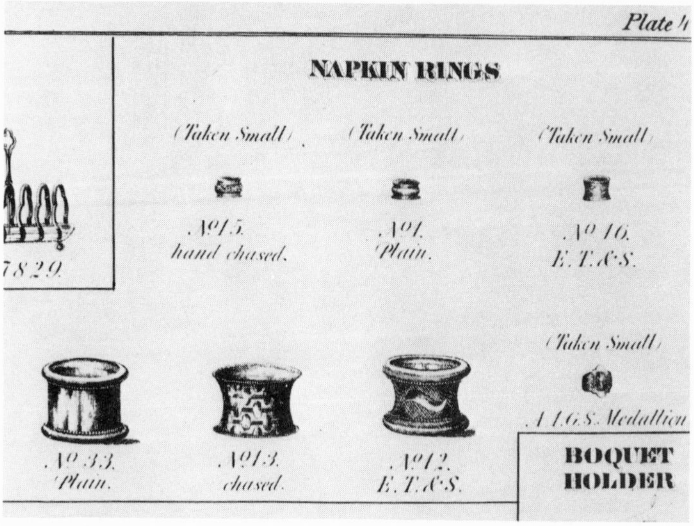

FIG. 37 *Napkin rings appear to have been an invention of the nineteenth century, their first mention in household manuals probably occurring in 1838. The 1868 catalog of J. F. Curran and Company showed only seven rather chaste napkin rings.*

Paintings through the centuries show napkins in use, but napkin rings are not mentioned in the literature until 1838 in *Work-Woman's Guide,* an English publication devoted to needlework. Directions were given for knitted napkin rings stiffened with wire or buckram. By the 1850s, napkin rings were made in both silverplate and sterling, though throughout the rest of the nineteenth century the greatest number of them—particularly the figural types—were of silverplate.

The Meriden Britannia Company catalog of 1860 listed 3 styles of napkin rings in its line, but did not illustrate them. By the 1867 catalog, 15 styles were illustrated, chiefly fairly simple rings whose decoration consisted of beading, engine-turning, engraving, and applied medallions. New York City silverplate manufacturer J. F. Curran and Company's 1868 catalog illustrated only 7 (fig. 37). Twelve years later, Meriden Britannia's 1879 catalog illustrated 40 styles on six pages (fig. 38). Of these, 19 had figures or raised ornaments—the first time such rings were shown. The 1886 catalog showed 86 styles, 35 of them figural. Reed and Barton devoted even more attention to the form: its 1877 catalog showed 51 styles, and its 1885

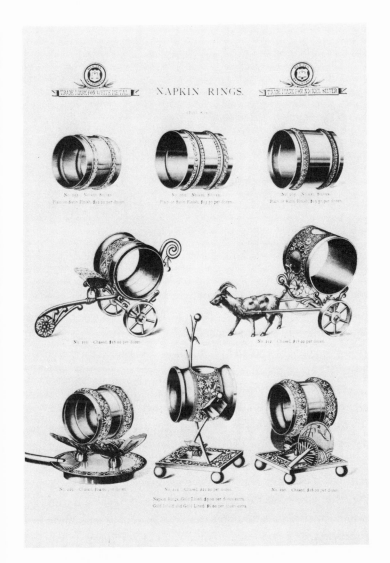

FIG. 38 *By the 1870s, napkin rings, usually made of silverplate, were available in a wide array of styles. The 1879 Meriden Britannia Company catalog may have been the first instance in which figural rings were illustrated. This page is one of six in that catalog devoted to napkin rings.*

catalog showed 129, 43 of them figural. After the 1880s, though, the appearance of napkin rings in catalogs fell off sharply; silverplated napkin rings almost disappeared by the early 1900s, when they were replaced by rings made of celluloid. Yet figural napkin rings are strictly American in origin,

FIG. 39 *These silverplated napkin rings, all produced by American silver manufacturers, date between 1866 and 1900 and show the favored decorative motifs of animals and children.*

frequently sporting motifs of animals and children at play (fig. 39). Sometimes napkin rings were manufactured with small glass bud vases attached; others were attached to individual casters, to a small butter plate, or to a vinegar condiment bottle.

The silverplated multiwalled ice water pitcher was another product of the Victorian age, and one that disappeared from sideboards at about the same time that caster sets began to decline in popularity. Yet the reason for the ephemeral success of the ice water pitcher is easier to discern: by the twentieth century, mechanical refrigeration made them unnecessary.

At the time of its invention in the 1850s, however, the multiwalled pitcher was an ingenious way of providing and maintaining a cool supply of drinking water. The numerous patents taken out for them and the space that manufacturers devoted to them in catalogs attest their great popularity. The first patent for such a pitcher was granted in the name of James Stimpson of Baltimore, Maryland, in 1854, and was actually issued to his son and executor, James H. Stimpson (fig. 40). Stimpson's pitcher had an inner lining of metal, with a space between the lining and the outer body for insulation (fig. 41). Later patents

FIG. 40 *James Stimpson's 1854 patent illustration for an ice water pitcher shows an inner lining of metal and a space between the lining and the outer body for insulation. The multiwalled pitcher became a central feature on Victorian sideboards.*

FIG. 41 *Meriden Britannia Company made this silverplated, double-walled pitcher around 1867.*

covered porcelain linings, and some also advertised "treble-walled" construction. Ice water pitchers were also made that tilted on elaborate stands, which often also held matching silverplated goblets and a waste bowl (fig. 42). In 1861 Meriden Britannia offered fourteen styles. As did other silverplated wares, the ice water pitcher reached the height of its stylistic diversity in the mid-1880s, when Meriden Britannia offered fifty-seven styles and Reed and Barton offered fifty-one (fig. 43a and b). Thereafter their number decreases markedly: only fourteen styles were offered by Reed and Barton in 1896, and practically none appears after 1900.

By the 1920s, less formal kinds of entertaining had affected the diversity and sheer array of silverplated tablewares used at the dinners of the American middle class. By 1965, a brochure advertising Reed and Barton's 1907 "Francis I" pattern showed only "the ten most essential serving pieces" out of the original set of seventy-seven pieces. As we look around the dining room of today, rarely do we see napkin rings, caster sets,

FIG. 43a and b *Simpson Hall, Miller and Company offered an array of styles in tilting ice water pitchers in its 1887 catalog, all with gold-lined cups and slop bowls.*

cake baskets, epergnes, revolving butter dishes, pickle jars, table bells, soup tureens, silver rests for the carving knife, silver points to hold corn cobs, finger bowls with doilies on a silver tray, salt spoons and open salt cellars, or table crumbers. Indeed, many Americans today set no table at all in the sense that the Victorians did—always, and necessarily, an elegant table with matched tablewares set in well-defined locations on the cloths, and with utensils for every conceivable function.

Contributors

CLIFFORD E. CLARK, JR., is the M.A. and A.D. Hulings Professor of American Studies at Carleton College, where he has taught since 1970. He is the author of *Henry Ward Beecher: Spokesman for a Middle-Class America,* published by the University of Illinois Press in 1978, and of *The American Family Home,* published by the University of North Carolina Press in 1986. He has written articles and essays on American nineteenth-century domestic architecture and religion and received his doctorate in history from Harvard University.

ELEANOR T. FORDYCE of Rochester, New York, began in 1954 to collect nineteenth-century cookbooks written and published in the United States. She has since amassed a collection of nearly 700 volumes and has lectured often on what cookbooks reveal about American cooking practices and culinary predilections.

JOHN F. KASSON has been teaching at the University of North Carolina since 1971 and is currently professor of history and adjunct professor of American studies. He received his doctorate in American studies from Yale University in 1971. He is author of *Civilizing the Machine: Technology and Republican Values in America, 1776–1900* and *Amusing the Million: Coney Island at the Turn of the Century.* He is now at work on a book about nineteenth-century urban America's manners.

DAVID W. MILLER has operated his own design firm since 1970 and has developed houseware designs for Revere Copper and Brass, Inc., Benjamin-Medwin, Inc., and Miller-Wescott, Inc., for which he designed plastic food forms in ten historical patterns. He has written and lectured on Victorian food molds, the crafting of historic molds, and historic molded foods.

DOROTHY T. RAINWATER is the author of six books on American and other silver: *American Silver Manufacturers,* her first, grew out of her work documenting silver in the collections of the Bernice P. Bishop Museum in Honolulu. She has done graduate work in decorative arts and interior design and has lectured and written frequently on American silver, particularly that of the Victorian era.

WILLIAM J. RORABAUGH is the author of *The Alcoholic Republic, an American Tradition,* published by Oxford University Press in 1979, and of *The Craft Apprentice: From Franklin to the Machine Age in America,* published by Oxford in 1986. Since 1976 he has been a professor of American history at the University of Washington.

SUSAN R. WILLIAMS is curator of household accessories and tablewares at the Strong Museum and author of *Savory Suppers and Fashionable Feasts: Dining in Victorian America,* published by Pantheon Books and the Strong Museum in 1986.

Index